Supporting and Accommodating Students with Special Health Care Needs

SPECIAL EDUCATION LAW, POLICY, AND PRACTICE

Series Editors
Mitchell L. Yell, PhD, University of South Carolina
David F. Bateman, PhD, American Institutes for Research

The Special Education Law, Policy, and Practice series highlights current trends and legal issues in the education of students with disabilities. The books in this series link legal requirements with evidence-based instruction and highlight practical applications for working with students with disabilities. The titles in the Special Education Law, Policy, and Practice series are designed not only to be required textbooks for general education and special education preservice teacher education programs but are also designed for practicing teachers, education administrators, principals, school counselors, school psychologists, parents, and others interested in improving the lives of students with disabilities. The Special Education Law, Policy, and Practice series is committed to research-based practices working to provide appropriate and meaningful educational programming for students with disabilities and their families.

Titles in the Series

The Essentials of Special Education Law by Andrew M. Markelz and David F. Bateman

Developing Educationally Meaningful and Legally Sound IEPs by Mitchell L. Yell, David F. Bateman, and James G. Shriner

Sexuality Education for Students with Disabilities edited by Thomas C. Gibbon, Elizabeth A. Harkins Monaco, and David F. Bateman

Creating Positive Elementary Classrooms: Preventing Behavior Challenges to Promote Learning by Stephen W. Smith and Mitchell L. Yell

Service Animals in Schools: Legal, Educational, Administrative, and Strategic Handling Aspects by Anne O. Papalia, Kathy B. Ewoldt, and David F. Bateman

Evidence-Based Practices for Supporting Individuals with Autism Spectrum Disorder edited by Laura C. Chezan, Katie Wolfe, and Erik Drasgow

Dispute Resolution Under the IDEA: Understanding, Avoiding, and Managing Special Education Disputes by David F. Bateman, Mitchell L. Yell, and Jonas Dorego

Advocating for the Common Good: People, Politics, Process, and Policy on Capitol Hill by Jane E. West

Related Services in Special Education: Working Together as a Team by Lisa Goran and David F. Bateman

The Essentials of Special Education Advocacy by Andrew M. Markelz, Sarah A. Nagro, Kevin Monnin, and David F. Bateman

Disability and Motor Behavior: A Handbook of Research edited by Ali S. Brian and Pamela S. Beach

You're Hired! Practical Strategies for Guiding Individuals with Autism Spectrum Disorder to Competitive Employment by Patricia S. Arter, Tammy B. H. Brown, and Jennifer Barna

Unraveling Dyslexia: A Guide for Teachers and Families by Kristin L. Sayeski

Supporting and Accommodating Students with Special Health Care Needs edited by Azure D. S. Angelov and Mary Jo Rattermann

Supporting and Accommodating Students with Special Health Care Needs

Edited by
Azure D. S. Angelov, PhD
and
Mary Jo Rattermann, PhD

ROWMAN & LITTLEFIELD
Lanham • Boulder • New York • London

Published by Rowman & Littlefield
An imprint of The Rowman & Littlefield Publishing Group, Inc.
4501 Forbes Boulevard, Suite 200, Lanham, Maryland 20706
www.rowman.com

86-90 Paul Street, London EC2A 4NE

Copyright © 2024 by The Rowman & Littlefield Publishing Group, Inc.

All rights reserved. No part of this book may be reproduced in any form or by any electronic or mechanical means, including information storage and retrieval systems, without written permission from the publisher, except by a reviewer who may quote passages in a review.

British Library Cataloguing in Publication Information Available

Library of Congress Cataloging-in-Publication Data

Names: Angelov, Azure, 1963– editor. | Rattermann, Mary Jo, 1962– editor.
Title: Supporting and accommodating students with special health care needs / Edited by Azure D. S. Angelov, PhD and Mary Jo Rattermann, PhD.
Description: Lanham, Maryland : Rowman & Littlefield, [2024] | Series: Special education law, policy, and practice | Includes bibliographical references and index.
Identifiers: LCCN 2023037009 (print) | LCCN 2023037010 (ebook) | ISBN 9781538170052 (hardback) | ISBN 9781538170069 (paperback) | ISBN 9781538170076 (epub)
Subjects: LCSH: Students with disabilities—Education. | Individualized education programs. | Special education—Curriculum. | Students with disabilities—Health and hygiene. | Students with disabilities—Services for. | Education and state.
Classification: LCC LC4065 .S87 2024 (print) | LCC LC4065 (ebook) | DDC 378.1/61—dc23/eng/20230828
LC record available at https://lccn.loc.gov/2023037009
LC ebook record available at https://lccn.loc.gov/2023037010

Contents

Editors' Note   vii

1   Students with Medical Issues and Individualized Education Programs   1
     Azure D. S. Angelov and Mary Jo Rattermann

2   Utilization of Health Data as Part of a Multiple Tiered Systemic Approach: The Journey to Leverage ESSA and Data to Inform Early Intervention Decision Making   15
     Azure D. S. Angelov, Mary Jo Rattermann, Thomas Reddicks, and Jessica Monk

3   A Schoolwide Approach to Health Care: An Urban School's Journey   27
     Shy-Quon Ely II and Nadia Miller

4   The Role of Health in Schools: MTSS Approach and Machine Learning Risk Levels   39
     Carolyn Gentle-Genitty, Francis Bowen, Christopher Kearney, Marlin Jackson, and Nathan Lashbrook

5   Lessons Learned by Leading during COVID   61
     Allison Arnold-Kempers, Matthew Wojas, Alyssa Preddie Allen, Denver Wade, and Sara Lauerman

6   The Educational Needs of Students with Chronic Illness   87
     Kristin Wikel and Andrew M. Markelz

7 School Nurses: Partners in Educating Students with Health
  Concerns and Special Needs   109
  Andrea Tanner and Cindy Hill

8 Recovery High Schools: Working at the Intersection of Education,
  Mental Health, and Addiction Science   129
  Linda Gagyi and Rachelle Gardner

Index   147

About the Editors   153

Editors' Note

Even before COVID-19, schools were increasingly responding to the impact and prevalence of special health care needs among children and youth. COVID-19 just brought the health needs of many students to the forefront. We need to learn from the past few years and plan for working with students with health needs. Many of these students with health needs are eligible for special education and related services and will need programming appropriate to address their unique needs. Further, school teams and special education personnel must continually ensure that goals and services within an IEP consider the student's individual circumstances and impact on functioning. This book will provide strategies for supporting students with health care needs with a more comprehensive approach to special education that fully embraces the opportunities of the health care sector, including referral, family engagement, report writing, IEP design, and implementation. Fortunately, school teams can apply many components of a health care needs approach to developing IEPs, regardless of the concern or the existence of a medical history.

Chapter 1

Students with Medical Issues and Individualized Education Programs

Azure D. S. Angelov and Mary Jo Rattermann

This chapter discusses students with medical and/or health issues and their resulting individualized education programs (IEPs), their definition, and their components, all the while focusing on the role of the teacher. It concludes with a checklist that will help a general or special education teacher before an IEP meeting determine the health care needs of a student and the supports that are necessary.

ELIGIBILITY

Not all students with medical and/or health needs are eligible for special education. In order to be eligible for special education one needs to require the services of a special education teacher. Students who require the services of a special education teacher are those who require specially designed instruction, materials, equipment, and other accommodations in order to make adequate academic progress and/or to develop and maintain appropriate behavior.

    (c)   Procedures for determining eligibility and educational need.

          (1)   In interpreting evaluation data for the purpose of determining if a child is a child with a disability under §300.8, and the educational needs of the child, each public agency must—

               (i)   Draw upon information from a variety of sources, including aptitude and achievement tests, parent input, and teacher recommendations, as well as information about the child's physical condition, social or cultural background, and adaptive behavior; and

(ii) Ensure that information obtained from all of these sources is documented and carefully considered.

(2) If a determination is made that a child has a disability and needs special education and related services, an IEP must be developed for the child in accordance with §§300.320 through 300.324. (Authority: 20 U.S.C. 1414(b)(4) and (5))

The important part of the definition provided here is that the student has a disability *and* needs special education and related services. There are some students with medical and/or health needs who *do not* require the services of a special education teacher. These students would receive a Section 504 plan that would provide accommodations for their disability.

WHAT IS SECTION 504?

Section 504 is a nondiscrimination law included in the Rehabilitation Act of 1973. It extends to individuals with disabilities the same kinds of protections Congress extended to people discriminated against because of race and sex. Common disabilities receiving Section 504 plans in schools include ADHD/ADD, nut allergies, asthma, and diabetes. This is important as many students with medical and/or health issues require the accommodations included in Section 504.[1]

More important points on Section 504:

1. Section 504 is an antidiscrimination law. There are no federal funds provided to school districts for the implementation of this law.
2. The responsibility not to discriminate against individuals with disabilities applies to all school personnel. It is not just students with disabilities who cannot be discriminated against; it is also parents and employees.
3. General education programs and teachers have the primary responsibility for the implementation of Section 504. Staff from special education may be consulted, but they do not have responsibility for implementation of the accommodations for the student.
4. The accommodations required by Section 504 apply to the entire school. This includes parents and visitors to events.

---

1. For more information on how to write a Section 504 plan, the reader is referred to https://www.psea.org/contentassets/ac6695903bd94d27aa14e85c3a12d90e/504-accommodations-guide.pdf.

WHAT IS A 504 PLAN?

Similar in idea to an IEP, the Section 504 plan lists the accommodations an eligible student would receive. See the list of possible accommodations below for examples. A Section 504 plan is individualized to the student and is based on the specific needs of the student's disability. Because a student who is eligible for a Section 504 plan will receive these services through general education programs or general education funded programs, it is very important that the general education teacher be a part of and understand the specific components of the plan.

Who Qualifies for a Section 504 Plan?

Any person who has a physical or mental impairment that substantially limits one or more major life activities (learning is considered a major life activity), has a record of such impairment, or is regarded as having such an impairment 29 U.S.C. § 794(a)(1996).

WHAT IS AN IEP?

An IEP, or individualized education program, is the written plan for the next year that provides the services offered to eligible students that is different than the general education program. IEPs are only provided to students eligible for special education and related services. It is a formal document that is only developed after a student has been declared eligible for special education and related services by a multidisciplinary team. For some students with medical and/or health issues this may come shortly after their diagnosis. For all eligible students the IEP is a legal document and is a contract between the school and the parent outlining what services will be provided.

PURPOSE OF THE IEP

The IEP document itself is very important. It is where the plan that the team has developed is documented. This document can be used for several purposes. They are not necessarily separate from each other, and in many ways are linked together. The IEP serves as a communication, evaluation, management, accountability, compliance, and monitoring document. Most importantly, however, is that it is a contract listing off the services a student will receive.

As a contract the IEP is a legally binding document and should be viewed as such between the school district and the parents. Schools must implement the services that are written in the IEP. This means that if the IEP team determined a student, due to their medical and/or health needs, requires special transportation to and from school, it would be listed in the IEP, and a school district must then provide it. If that does not happen, the district would then be violating the contract and giving the parent rights to file litigation through a due process hearing. The same goes if a student is expected to receive accommodations and special education services for easy access to a bathroom and either the school district does not provide it or is only providing it occasionally: the school has violated the contract. Should the district fail to provide what is listed in the IEP, the parents can file litigation to get back services provided.

It is important to point out that contracts can change, as long as both parties (school district and parents) agree to the changes. This is important especially as a student's medical and/or health needs may change over the course of the year. However, if there is no agreement to make changes, the contract as originally written stands and there can be no changes unless a due process hearing rules otherwise (Yell, Bateman, & Shriner, 2022).

Description and Purpose of the Required Components

IEPs are getting longer, and this is important with all the medical and/or health needs students are presenting in schools. The following will highlight the specific components of the IEP and describe their purposes. Just a reminder that the IEP serves as an important communication tool for the school staff and parents, so that informed educational decisions can be made.

The following section will list the components of the IEP and give a brief description of the rationale for that component. This section includes components that are both mandated by the federal regulations and are ones typically found in most state IEPs.

Demographics—This section documents information about the student that includes name, date of birth, age, grade, anticipated year of graduation, school district, parents' names, address, phone number, and disability category.

IEP Team Signatures—This section is where team members sign that they were in attendance and participated in the IEP meeting.

Special Factors—These are questions that are typically asked at the first part of the IEP meeting. If any of these questions are answered in the affirmative, there needs to be programming related to that issue included in the IEP. These questions include:

1. Is the student blind or visually impaired?
2. Is the student deaf or hard of hearing?
3. Does the student have communication needs?
4. Does the student require assistive technology devices or services?
5. Does the student have limited English proficiency?
6. Does the student exhibit behaviors that impede his/her learning or that of others?

Present Levels of Academic Achievement and Functional Performance—For students with medical and/or health needs this is where the important and specific information about their needs is to be listed. All services, goals, objectives, and placements are based on this information. This section should also provide a summary of the student's performance in their current educational program and this should indicate the student's instructional and functional levels. It should include information regarding classroom performance and the results of any academic achievement or functional performance assessments that have been administered. It is important to point out that information contained in this section provides baseline data for developing the IEP and making all programmatic determinations (Yell, Bateman, & Shriner, 2022). The information in this section should consider the most recent results of the initial multidisciplinary team report or the triennial evaluation, information from medical and/or health providers, results of curriculum-based assessments, and results of ongoing progress monitoring, why it is important that the student improve in this area, and how their performance compares to that of their peers.

Goals and Objectives—Annual goals are measurable statements describing what a student should be able to accomplish over a calendar year. These statements will include specifics about the behaviors you want the student to perform (reading, math, handwriting, functional performance, speech, etc.) and how well you want the student to perform these actions. There needs to be a clear and direct link between the student's present level statement (described earlier) and the goals and objectives.

The IEP should include how often progress is going to be monitored and how often the reports will be provided to the parents on the status of the goals and objectives. Parents need to receive progress notes on the IEP goals at least as often as general education parents receive report cards.

Accommodations and/or Modifications—This section details any adaptation to content, methodology, or the delivery of instruction assisting the student in meeting their goals. It is expected the IEP team would develop this based on the individual needs of the student with consideration given to how their disability impacts their ability to perform. This is a very important section for the general education teacher because you will be implementing and giving much input on what is to be included in this section. For students with medical and/or health needs this section would list the specific information that teachers, bus drivers, classroom aides, and others need to know and describe how and when the accommodations should be provided.

SUPPORTS FOR THE GENERAL EDUCATION TEACHER IN THE IEP

General education teachers providing support to students with medical and/or health needs may require assistance in implementing the IEP. The teacher may need help with implementing bathroom breaks, positioning in the classroom, and designing and implementing appropriate accommodations. Teachers may need to help the family with technology and strategies to use at home when there are health care needs to be addressed that require the student to miss school. This section of the IEP provides an opportunity for the team to discuss and articulate those specific supports or training necessary for school personnel to provide free appropriate public education (FAPE).

This could include:

- *Aids*—learning aids or behavioral tracking aids provided to help the student to make it through the day.
- *Training*—workshops on the specific health care needs or new ways to take data on the students so others can help plan.
- *Equipment*—equipment for remote instruction, apps for mobile devices that help take data, or adaptive equipment that helps the student participate in the classroom.

For each form of support listed here, the IEP should list the school personnel to receive the support, the support, and the location and the frequency of the support to be provided. Location refers to where school personnel will be receiving the support. Frequency refers to how often school personnel will be receiving the support. The projected beginning date and the anticipated duration of the support must be listed. Duration refers to the anticipated ending date for support.

Related Services—Many students with medical and/or health needs require more assistance than what can be provided by a teacher alone. They may need speech therapy, occupational therapy, physical therapy, or assistance in attending school remotely. If the IEP team determines the student has a need for a related service, the specifics of the frequency, location, and duration of the service, along with the beginning and ending dates of the service, will be included here.

Placement—The information in the PLAAFP statement of the IEP determine the goals and objectives that must be addressed. The detail and time involved in addressing these goals and objectives determines the location of the services the student is to receive. Special education is a service, not a place. Importantly, the needs of the student dictate the services to be provided, not what happens to be available in the district. Additionally, for students with medical and/or health needs, school districts may have to make changes to the level of assistance provided as the student's needs change over time.

Role of the Teacher in IEP Development

Either a special education teacher or a special education administrator typically writes the IEPs. They gather and compile information from team members and write it into the document. They should work to make sure they have the most recent medical and health information about the child. Teachers should be able to describe how the student is functioning in the classroom, accommodations that are working/not working, how the student interacts with peers, and also be the point person for communications with the parents.

LEAST RESTRICTIVE ENVIRONMENT

Least restrictive environment (LRE) is one of the main tenets of special education. Under LRE the presumption is students with disabilities will be educated in general education classrooms alongside their typically learning peers as much as possible and provided with the necessary supports and services to meet their needs (Yell, Bateman, & Shriner, 2022). For students with medical and/or health needs to participate fully, both academically and socially, schools will have to work to make necessary accommodations and not just assume the student needs to go to a more restrictive placement.

Students with medical and/or health needs are to be educated in the general education classroom until all available methods are tried to meet their needs in this environment. Only after every reasonable method is tried in the general education classroom and the needs of a student are still not met should the student be pulled out for additional services.

Examples of this include students with disabilities being briefly removed because they have missed a lot of school due to surgeries, and they need greater assistance to catch back up to their peers. Another example is students with anxiety issues being taught strategies for dealing with frustration and then going back to the general education classroom.

Nonexamples of this include placing a student in a special education class without even trying accommodations or automatically assuming he or she needs assistance just because of his or her disability. Case law on this is very specific that removal to a special education classroom is only done after other options have been tried. See, for example, *Daniel R. R. v. State Board of Education* (1989); *Oberti v. Board of Education of the Borough of Clementon School District* (1993); *Roncker v. Walter* (1983).

PARTICIPATION IN STATE AND DISTRICT ASSESSMENTS

The IEP team must determine appropriate and necessary accommodations for students with disabilities as a part of their participation with state- and districtwide assessments. The teacher often knows the student better than other members of the team and can advocate on their behalf. The IEP team will make the determination about a student's participation in academic courses and also the assessments that will be used.

For students who qualify to participate in an alternate assessment system, the IEP must contain an explanation of why the student cannot participate in the statewide assessments. The IEP also must explain why the alternative is an appropriate assessment for the student.

Reevaluation

IEP teams must consider if a reevaluation is needed at least once every three years or more frequently if either needed or the parent or teacher requests it. Students with medical and/or health needs who have changes to their needs or episodic events may require a more frequent reevaluation. For students with medical and/or health needs the reevaluation has three purposes:

- To determine whether the student remains eligible for special education services.
- To ensure the individual needs of a student with a disability are identified.
- To gather information that is necessary for appropriate educational programming.

The team may determine that additional information is needed for program planning and not have to go through the formal reevaluation process (Yell, Bateman, & Shriner, 2022). The primary purposes of a reevaluation are to determine whether or not the student is still eligible for special education services. The decision must be documented. More testing may be necessary to help make this determination. The team needs to make sure it has recent medical and/or health data on the student to help make an informed decision about services.

STANDARDS-BASED IEPS

There is increasing discussion about standards-based IEPs. A standards-based IEP determines how a student is currently performing compared to expected performance on grade-level academic standards. The focus of the IEP is to bridge the gap and to raise the student's level of functioning to grade level. The belief is that a standards-based IEP better helps students stay on track for their grade. Standards-based IEPs can help everyone plan for instruction that will move the student toward grade level. This encourages everyone to work together to figure out what can be done to get the student up to grade level. However, using grade-level standards to establish IEP goals can ignore the individual needs of a student. Additionally, if a student is functioning much below grade level, it would be very difficult to move a student to grade level within the one-year duration of the IEP. Standards-based IEP goals need to be realistic as well as ambitious (Yell, Bateman, & Shriner, 2022).

IMPORTANT IEP POINTS FOR STUDENTS WITH MEDICAL AND/OR HEALTH NEEDS

Classroom teachers will have a vital role in the implementation of a student's IEP. There is a lot of information about IEPs in this chapter. Seven very important points stand, however.

First, the most important part of the IEP is the present level statement. It is vital to have updated medical and/or health information in this section so the team can review the current needs of the student and make informed decisions about what services are needed.

Second, for students with medical and/or health needs, it is important to note that the IEP is not a fixed document and that changes will possibly be needed as the student's condition changes throughout the year. It is imperative that families keep the school team informed about changes to the student's status. Teachers may notice problems before others and can call for a new IEP meeting to discuss issues at any time.

Third, the services of the student are to be provided in accordance with their medical and/or health needs, not what happens to be available within the district. The student's needs dictate the services, not the other way around. For some students with rare disabilities or health conditions it is important to pay close attention to the needs the student has and obtain assistance from experts when needed.

Fourth, it is very important for school officials to preserve confidentiality with all the information that will be shared about the student. All staff are legally required to maintain confidentiality and to only talk with others who need to know about the student.

Fifth, the student needs to be treated as an individual. There are no average students with medical and/or health needs. The student does not choose to have this issue. Teachers need to work with students to provide assistance and all the necessary supports so that they make progress in the curriculum.

Sixth, all students who only receive a Section 504 plan because they do not require special education should be closely monitored to make sure they continually do not need additional assistance. All new information provided should be reviewed with that in mind.

Seventh, teachers of students with medical and health needs should expect and plan for frequent and sometimes prolonged absences from school. Teachers should prepare work for the student to complete while they are at home but be reasonable about expectations for completion and quality. Students who require prolonged hospitalization may receive instruction through a hospital-based teacher. Collaboration between the classroom teacher and the hospital teacher can help to ensure a smooth transition back into the classroom once the student is discharged.

CHAPTER SUMMARY

For most students with medical and/or health needs, teachers spend the most time with the students and get to observe their academic, social, functional, and behavioral strengths and needs more regularly. Because of this, teachers have important knowledge about content, what goes on in the classroom, the pace of lessons, instruction provided, and information on state standards. Students may need greater assistance sometimes compared to others.

Teachers are expected to provide descriptions of services, adaptations, and modifications required to help the student as well as recommendations and feedback regarding the development of the IEP. Related services personnel often only see the student for a short time each week. The teacher should work to meet with the related services personnel to make sure they understand how the student is doing in the classroom and be able to help plan with implementation of strategies.

REFERENCES

Daniel R. R. v. State Board of Education, 874 F. 2d 1036 (5th Cir. 1989).
Individuals with Disabilities Education Act, 20 U.S.C. § 300.1.et. seq.
Oberti v. Board of Education of the Borough of Clementon School District, 995 F.2d 1024 (3rd Cir. 1993).
Roncker v. Walter, 700 F.2d 1058 (6th Cir. 1983).
Yell, M. L. (2020). *The law and special education.* Fifth edition. Pearson.
Yell, M. L., Bateman, D. F., & Shriner, J. (2022). *Developing educationally meaningful and legally sound IEPs.* Rowman & Littlefield.

APPENDIX

Health Level of Supports

Name: _____

Age: _____

Grade Level: _____

Disability(ies): _____

Primary Support: _____

Related Services: _____

School: _____

Date of Last IEP Revision: _____

Level of Support: _____
(Check all that apply to the student's needs in the school setting.)

Health support—The student needs this type of aide, in accordance with a health services plan, to:

☐ Monitor for seizure activity, vital signs, other medical symptoms, or drug side effects. Describe the nature of the activity or symptom for which monitoring will be required and, if possible, the actual or expected frequency of such activity or symptoms:

_____
_____
_____

☐ Implement emergency medical procedures pending arrival of nurse.
☐ Monitor or make routine adjustments to equipment. Describe the equipment in question:

_____

☐ Assist with toileting or self-care.
☐ Assist with feeding.
☐ Assist with mobility (wheelchair, walker, lift, positioning).
☐ Other (describe):

_____
_____
_____

Specific training needed:

_____
_____
_____
_____
_____
_____
_____

Next steps and who is responsible:

Step to Be Taken:	**Responsible Party:**

Note: This form is from Yell, Bateman, & Shriner (2022).

School Day Needs Assessment

Directions: Review the student's entire school day and determine specifically what the student can or cannot do and the extent he/she needs assistance.

Activity	*What student can do without assistance*	*What student cannot do and needs accommodations to complete*	*What student cannot do and needs assistance with*	*Identify areas to promote social acceptance and how peers will be utilized*	*Identify areas you will target for independence (should be identified in IEP)*

Chapter 2

Utilization of Health Data as Part of a Multiple Tiered Systemic Approach

The Journey to Leverage ESSA and Data to Inform Early Intervention Decision Making

Azure D. S. Angelov, Mary Jo Rattermann, Thomas Reddicks, and Jessica Monk

Utilization of health data in the educational space has historically been limited to students with individualized education plans (IEP) or 504 plans. This chapter explores the journey of one charter school as they unexpectedly design, develop, implement, evaluate, and expand a multitiered systemic system of support (MTSS) utilizing social determinants of health data collected by the school nurse. A new quantitative academic indicator, the Academic Health Cliff, is introduced as part of the research methodology. The dataset shared is part of a multiple year longitudinal study at one charter school site. The chapter specifically shares data collected during the 2019–2020 school year, the school year of the COVID-19 quarantine, and the 2020–2021 school year following. Specific attention is given to more fully understanding the ability of charter schools to foster emerging educational innovation, new opportunities within the existing MTSS process to utilize health data for academic decision making, and the importance of sharing evidence-based best practices to the larger educational community to support COVID recovery efforts. Recommendations for future research efforts are discussed.

SPECIAL EDUCATION INNOVATION AND RESEARCH IN CHARTER SCHOOLS

Ray Budde's "Education by Charter" (1988, although he first presented the concept a decade earlier, to the Society for General Systems Research) recommended a restructuring of the traditional public school district by allowing groups of teachers to start autonomous "charter schools" within existing districts, hence a decentralized model of public education. One of the pillars of the charter movement has been the opportunity for charter schools to be places where master teachers could implement innovative educational models and ideas. In much the same way that university-based schools of education would partner with a traditional public school district to create laboratory (lab) schools to engage in research, charter schools were envisioned to be a place that educators would be empowered to explore various aspects of the profession for the betterment of all educational practice (Budde, 1988).

For those educators focused on equitable practices, ensuring that our most vulnerable students are receiving high-quality services is an important indicator of success for the school choice movement. It's also important to acknowledge that as a field, special education specifically needs to move past opinions about the school choice movement and toward a scientific approach to understanding what is emerging from charter school practice. After completing a study focused on special education services being provided in charter schools in Indianapolis, Indiana University professor Hardy Murphy shared, "It's time to move beyond the debate about whether or not charter schools are effective and start talking about, when they are effective, why, and for whom," adding that successful approaches can be used in other settings (News at IU: Law and Policy, 2019).

Murphy isn't the first member of the higher education community to note the need to study emerging practices specific to special education within the Indianapolis charter community. Dr. Robin Lake of the University of Washington recently (DeArmond et al., 2019) shared, "About 14 percent of those enrolled in Indy charter schools are students with special needs, compared to 18 percent in the Indianapolis Public Schools. Too many charter schools in the city are good enough to be renewed but lack incentive and knowledge to continue to innovate for instructional improvements."

This chapter strives to begin to answer these calls by sharing the experiences of one Indianapolis charter school that has designed and developed an MTSS process that incorporates social determinants of health data collected during visits to the school nurse's office in the academic intervention decision-making process. While health data has been leveraged on behalf of children with IEP and 504 plans for educational planning and decision making, it has never been leveraged in a quantifiable way to impact academic achievement of students who do not qualify as 504 or for an IEP.

GEI TO RTI TO MTSS: AN EVOLVING APPROACH

Special education as a field has evolved in its approach to identification and supporting students without overrepresenting African American males.

In the late 1990s schools began to implement General Education Intervention (GEI) under the Elementary and Secondary Education Act (ESEA). In a response to the overwhelming amount of data that emerged on the number of African American males inappropriately placed in special education programs, schools were required to put rudimentary and locally chosen screening tools in place prior to fully testing a student for special education services. In the early 2000s GEI took a more data-driven approach under the No Child Left Behind Act (NCLB) and schools began to implement Response To Intervention (RTI).

RTI processes pushed schools to use data in their decision making and to take a "tiered" approach to providing academic support. Specific attention was paid to literacy to ensure that academics were at the forefront of decision making and implementation of supports. In December 2015, Congress enacted the Every Student Succeeds Act (ESSA). ESSA moved schools from being required to use any data to using valid and reliable data that was purposeful. Federal language shifted from NCLB's "data driven" to ESSA's "evidence based." In light of ESSA's more evidence-based approach to instruction and support, RTI began to evolve into MTSS in late 2015–2016. Per federal guidelines, MTSS is envisioned to:

1. "(III) implementation of a schoolwide tiered model to prevent and address problem behavior, and early intervening services, coordinated with similar activities and services carried out under the Individuals with Disabilities Education Act (20 U.S.C. 1400 et seq.)
2. "(F) developing programs and activities that increase the ability of teachers to effectively teach children with disabilities, including children with significant cognitive disabilities, and English learners, which may include the use of multi-tier systems of support and positive behavioral intervention and supports, so that such children with disabilities and English learners can meet the challenging State academic standards (20 U.S.C. 1400 et seq.)
3. "(33) MULTI-TIER SYSTEM OF SUPPORTS.—The term 'multitier system of supports' means a comprehensive continuum of evidence-based, systemic practices to support a rapid response to students' needs, with regular observation to facilitate data-based instructional decision-making" (20 U.S.C. 1400 et seq.).

Instead of only being tied to literacy data in a three-tiered approach, schools are now encouraged to be more inclusive of various forms of valid and reliable data that help inform educational decision making. Standardized test scores are only meant to be one piece of the data that schools use to make decisions. This seismic policy shift from NCLB to ESSA has provided schools with far more autonomy and responsibility specific to how they use data to inform their instructional practice.

SOCIAL DETERMINANTS OF HEALTH DATA AND THE MTSS PROCESS

As urban and rural communities face health and academic issues emerging from the Coronavirus pandemic, toxic levels of lead in water and on playgrounds, and cancer-causing chemicals leaked into the sewer and drainage systems, the intersectionality of public education and private health care has begun to be more intertwined. By utilizing scientifically rigorous data collection protocols, we can begin to more closely tie the physical impact of poverty via social determinants of health definitions to effective evidence-based academic achievement supports.

Preliminary research on this specific approach to MTSS (Angelov et al., 2020a; Rattermann et al., 2021) has yielded statistically significant results specific to the predictive nature of social determinants of health data from the nurse's office and its ability to impact academic decision making for any student visiting the nurse's office. Additionally, school leadership has presented this process as an example of best practice at state, regional, and national conferences in efforts to disseminate the practice more broadly to the field (Angelov et al., 2020b; Reddicks, 2018; Reddicks & Monk, 2019; Reddicks et al., 2018). While previous research has focused on the student outcome aspect of this work, this chapter will focus on the importance of utilizing valid and reliable data specific to the social determinants of health as part of implementing this process within urban school contexts.

A CHARTER SCHOOL CONTEXT: FERTILE GROUNDS FOR INNOVATION TO GROW

Nowland Schools of Excellence (NSE) is a public urban charter school on the near eastside of Indianapolis. NSE serves students in grades K–8. With a diverse student body of more than one thousand students, NSE provides a sample of students who are navigating poverty—with 83 percent of students qualifying for free and reduced meals. The students at NSE are also ethnically diverse, with African American students making up 49 percent of NSE's population, while Latinos are 16 percent, multiracial students are 10 percent, and European American students are 25 percent. Almost 20 percent of NSE's students are identified as students with disabilities and receive special education services and 6 percent are identified as English language learners.

NSE is a high-performing school, with approximately 90 percent of all NSE students passing the state mandated IREAD 3 test and more than 80 percent of all NSE students passing both the English and math portions of the state-mandated ISTEP test during the years corresponding to the data being used in this research. NSE has also boasted the highest achievement of students with IEPs in the state for the past three years in a row (IDOE Compass, 2020). NSE has also garnered the attention of numerous professional organizations.

The National Center on Special Education in Charter Schools has honored NSE as a national center of excellence, the School Based Health Alliance made NSE their local site of excellence for their national conference held in Indianapolis in 2018, the Indiana Department of Education has named NSE a Four Star School, the Indianapolis Urban League honored NSE with the 2018 and 2019 school excellence award, and the US Department of Education has named NSE a National Blue Ribbon School and a 2020 Successful Charter School profile specifically for scaling and sustaining effective practices.

The leadership at NSE believe that there is an interaction between health, poverty, and education that impacts overall health and wellness of students living in urban areas that navigate poverty. In 2008, the World Health Organization defined social determinants of health as "conditions in which people are born, grow, live, work, and age" and "the fundamental drivers of these conditions." The American Public Health Association (2010) found that graduation from high school increased the average life span by nine years. Unfortunately, equitable access to high-quality health care for urban students navigating poverty is currently not a reality for many (American Public Health Association, 2010). Since 2013 NSE has been implementing the University of Tennessee's Consortium for Health Education, Economic Empowerment, and Research (CHEER) data collection protocols for all visits to their nurse's office. Triangulating this data with academic achievement and behavior data has provided the NSE staff with reliable data that allows them to provide academic supports earlier and more strategically.

METHODS

This study discusses one effective use of collecting, analyzing, and acting on data that has been collected using the CHEER platform. CHEER is a data-driven approach that integrates health, education, economic, and other social factors in a comprehensive tracking system developed by the University of Tennessee (Brickman, 2013). The purpose of CHEER is to help stakeholders that are involved in a child's development, including teachers, doctors, parents, and public agencies, to address factors that affect children's health and educational outcomes with friendly, accessible data. This data integration platform provides CHEER partners with longitudinally track function, such as guide intervention, referral information, and feedback system, to maximize children's health and education.

Since 2013 NSE has employed a full-time nurse, who during the time of the data collection saw seventy to one hundred students per day. These visits range from a student who is sick with the flu to a student who finds the class overwhelming and simply needs to talk to a sympathetic adult. The data was entered into the University of Tennessee's CHEER data collection platform, following the CHEER protocols for all visits to the nurse's office.

An example of student health data being used as part of the MTSS process can be seen in the Paramount Health Data Project (PHDP). PHDP provides support to schools by correlating student health data with academic achievement in order to identify students at risk of academic failure. PHDP supports all types of schools—K–12, private as well as traditional and nontraditional public, rural, suburban, and urban. A recent case study found PHDP working with a network of three charter schools on the near eastside of Indianapolis. These urban schools serve students in grades K–8 in three separate buildings: one K–8, one K–5, and one middle school that is housed in the same building as a project-based charter high school. All three schools serve a diverse student body, with a majority of students qualifying for free and reduced meals, a common indicator of poverty. These schools are also ethnically diverse, with African American students making up the majority of the student population across all three schools, and with Latino and multiracial and white students also making up sizeable portions of the student body. Almost 20 percent of students are identified as students with disabilities and receive special education services and 6 percent are identified as English language learners. The K–8 school, which is the school of interest in this case study, is the "flagship" campus of the three schools, having been established over ten years ago, while the two other schools are considerably newer. The K–8 school is considered a high-performing school, with approximately 90 percent of third-grade students passing the state mandated reading test and more than 80 percent of all students passing both the English and math portions of the state-mandated testing for the most recent valid testing years.

To examine the impact of student health on academic achievement a dataset was constructed from the 2019–2020 and 2020–2021 academic years that included student demographics such as gender, race/ethnicity and grade, the number of visits to the school nurse, and student scores on Cambium Clearsight, a standardized assessment of student academic achievement. Cambium

Clearsight was administered longitudinally at three time points of the year (that is, it was given at the beginning of the academic year [BOY], in the middle of the academic year [MOY], and near the end of the academic year [EOY] in two subject areas: mathematics and English language arts [ELA]). The student health data was collected by a full-time school nurse who was employed at the case study school. This nurse would often see from seventy to one hundred students per day, for reasons ranging from a student who is sick with the flu to a student who finds the class overwhelming and simply needs to talk to a sympathetic adult. The school nurse places these visits into one of the following categories:

- Dermatological (for example, rash, eczema, bug bite, splinter)
- Eye/ears/nose/throat (for example, earache, sore throat, pinkeye)
- Gastrointestinal (for example, heartburn, nausea, diarrhea)
- Neurological (for example, headache, dizziness, falling asleep in class)
- Parasites/infections (for example, bed bugs, head lice, ticks)
- Medication dosage
- Psychosocial (for example, anxiety, altercation, tearful, needs to talk)
- Respiratory (for example, choking, cough, shortness of breath)
- Other/miscellaneous (for example, physical injury, chills, illness)

Previous research has shown that there is a negative relationship between the number of visits to the school nurse and performance on tests of academic achievement (Rattermann et al., 2021). That is, a higher number of visits to the school nurse is predictive of lower scores on standardized academic achievement tests. This relationship between visits to the school nurse and lower academic achievement is indicative of overall poor health, and it is the student's poor health that is negatively impacting student academic performance.

While this is useful information for school leaders, this does not tell a school principal how to intercede on behalf of a student who may be at risk for academic failure. School leaders need specific information about students who are at risk—ideally, characteristics that will allow them to quickly identify these students and intervene with high-quality academic supports. To provide this type of actionable information, PHDP analyzes student health and academic achievement data and shares it with school leaders in an Academic Health Report Card. This report card includes a breakdown of student performance on a standardized academic assessment, such as Cambium Clearsight, at the beginning, middle, and end of the academic year by the type of visit to the school nurse. The academic assessment data is provided as an aggregate of ELA and math combined and also as separate measures. The amount of growth from the beginning of the year to the middle and the end of the year is also calculated. Additionally, the report includes the total number of visits to the school nurse broken down by type of visit, as well as all of the various indicators by gender and by race/ethnicity. In this way, a principal can see which type of complaints were most prevalent, which type of complaints were most predictive of lower test scores, and if there were any notable differences based on gender or race in the type of complaints from students in her school during the previous academic year.

Additional information is provided in the form of the Academic Health Score. The Academic Health Score reflects the overall health of the student body and is calculated by determining the Academic Health Cliff for that building. The Academic Health Cliff is based on the hypothesis that there are two groups of students in a school—*healthy students* and *students at risk based on health factors* that are often associated with *social determinants of health*.

To test this assumption, student health and student achievement data from the 2019–2020 academic year from the case study school were analyzed to determine the Academic Health Cliff. Using a process proprietary to PHDP, two groups of students were formed based on the number of visits to the school nurse over the course of the academic year and the aggregate of their ELA and math academic assessment scores from the EOY testing. These two pieces of data—one reflecting student health and one reflecting student academic success—were analyzed using a proprietary algorithm that groups data until the most efficient combinations of datapoints are formed. In the case of the Health Data Project, the relationships between the number of visits to the school nurse and student assessment data are detected and two groups are formed. These groups are based on the number of visits to the school nurse below which student academic performance is not negatively affected by student health and the number above which student academic performance is negatively impacted by student health: the Academic Health Cliff.

In the example of the NSE school, the grouping process resulted in an Academic Health Cliff value of 7, which means that the PHDP model found that students who showed significantly higher assessment scores—the "healthy students"—exhibited six or fewer visits to the school nurse office while the "students at risk" exhibited seven or more visits. Using the value of six or fewer as the basis, an Academic Health Score was calculated for the school based on the proportion of students in the previous year who had six or fewer visits to the school nurse. An examination of the data from the 2019–2020 school year found that 75 percent of students had visited the school nurse fewer than six times, while 25 percent had visited more, suggesting that they were at academic risk. As a test of the underlying logic of the Academic Health Cliff, the students were divided into the hypothesized

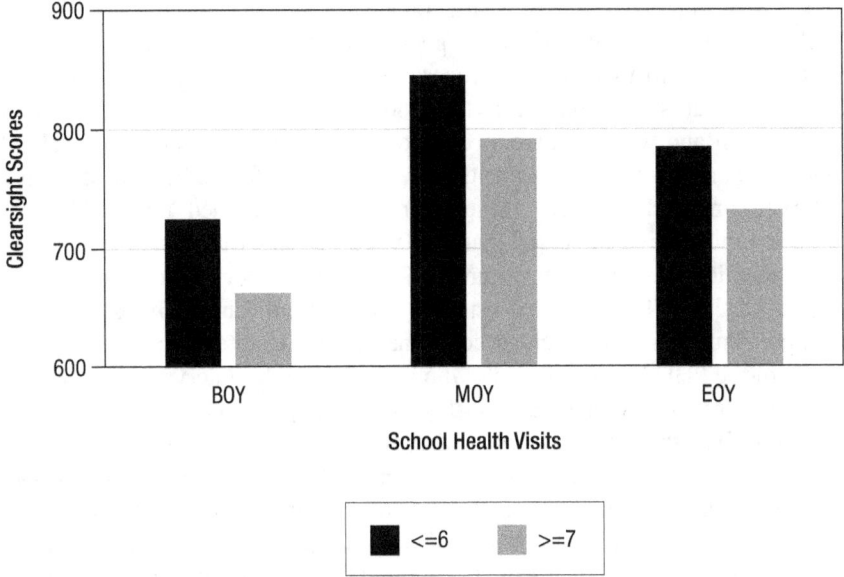

Figure 2.1. Health Visits and Academic Data from the NSE School

groups of "healthy students" with six or fewer visits and at-risk students of seven or more. The aggregate ELA and Math Clearsight testing data from the 2019–2020 school year was graphed and can be seen in figure 2.1. These data show that the healthy students' scores were significantly higher than those of the at-risk students at the BOY testing, with an independent samples t-test conforming that aggregate performance for the healthy students (M = 724, SD = 153) was significantly higher than that of the at-risk students (M = 660, SD = 136); (t(393) = 3.77, p < .001). The same pattern was found at the MOY testing and again at EOY testing: at MOY healthy students (M = 845, SD = 149) had higher aggregate scores than at-risk students (M = 793, SD = 132); (t(393) = 3.15, p < .001), and EOY healthy students (M = 787, SD = 149) had higher aggregate scores than at-risk students (M = 733, SD = 147); (t(393) = 3.28, p < .001).

ONE YEAR LATER: DATA FROM THE 2020–2021 SCHOOL YEAR

The goal of the Paramount Health Data Project is to provide MTSS teams with high-quality actionable student data that can be used to improve the educational outcomes of at-risk students. Based on the information provided to the NSE in the 2019–2020 Academic Health Report Card, the MTSS team included student health data, and specifically the concept of the Academic Health Cliff, into their MTSS process. Specifically, during the 2020–2021 academic year, student data from the school nurse was included in the MTSS data stream and when a student reached a total of seven visits to the school nurse, regardless of the reason, they were flagged for additional academic interventions and support. These interventions continued until additional progress monitoring indicated that they were no longer necessary.

Academic assessment data from the 2020–2021 academic year reveals the impact of the PHDP process on student achievement. The analyses presented compare students who received additional academic interventions solely because of the PHDP data—students who were flagged for intervention by PHDP but were already receiving additional academic supports due to the special education or English language learner status were not included in these analyses.

Comparisons were made between students who were flagged for additional academic supports and interventions due to the number of visits to the school nurse and those students at the school who did not need any additional interventions. Only student data from Cambium Clearsight for the MOY and EOY testing cycles were available for analysis, due to a different version of the test being administered during BOY testing. For these comparisons, student growth from the MOY to EOY testing cycle was calculated by subtracting each student's MOY Clearsight score from their EOY Clearsight score. Students who received additional supports due to the Health Data Project showed greater growth in mathematics ($M = 31.33$, $SD = 34.3$) than those students who did not need any additional interventions ($M = 24.57$, $SD = 26.4$), a difference that was found to be moderately significant by independent samples t-test ($t(187) = 1.29$, $p < .08$). The growth in ELA for Health Data Project students ($M = 29.11$, $SD = 45.82$), while in the right direction, was not significantly different from the growth in ELA Clearsight scores for students with no interventions ($M = 25.71$, $SD = 55.11$).

These results suggest that over the course of the 2020–2021 academic year, the interventions and supports provided to students based on their health had a significant impact on their mathematics assessment scores, with PHDP intervention students showing greater growth from MOY testing to EOY testing than students who did not require any additional academic interventions.

DISCUSSION

Master teachers and school leaders across the country are looking for innovative ways to support students as we enter the recovery phase of the

COVID-19 pandemic. It is unrealistic to believe that old solutions will solve new problems. The impact of the COVID-19 pandemic on the educational landscape is undeniable and will be felt for generations to come. While many schools struggle to differentiate between COVID learning loss and inappropriately placing students in special education programs, more robust and evidence-based models of MTSS are warranted. By introducing the concept of the Academic Health Cliff, this chapter pushes educators across the sector to reimagine how to incorporate health data in the academic decision-making process prior to providing a student with a 504 plan or an IEP. This type of proactive and evidence-based approach is necessary following the COVID-19 pandemic to ensure that reform efforts to combat the overrepresentation of students in special education programs are responsive to better understanding COVID learning loss versus actual cognitive disabilities.

The time has never been more opportune or necessary for educators to learn from each other. As charter schools become a more established member of the larger educational community, the reality of their ability to share emerging best practices has come of age. NSE's willingness to develop and scale a project of this scope is notable and admirable. Historically, a research project of this nature would come from a university or research center. Future research should focus on the supports necessary to build research capacity in charter schools as a way to share innovation emerging from this sector more broadly.

REFERENCES

American Public Health Association (2010). Public health and education: Working collaboratively across sectors to improve high school graduation as a means to eliminate health disparities. Policy Number: 2010.

Angelov, A. D., Bateman, D. F., Murado-Rhim, L., Reddicks, T., & Lancet, S. (2020a). Charter schools: An update. National Council for Exceptional Children Conference. Portland, OR.

Angelov, A. D., Pettinga, D., & Bateman, D. F. (2020b). The Paramount Health Data Project. In *Hashtags & headlines marketing for school leaders* (pp. 82–85). Lanham, MD: Rowman & Littlefield.

Brickman (2013). Imagine a community where children's health and education records are integrated and readily accessible for those who can best help children. Retrieved from https://www.newschallenge.org/challenge/healthdata/entries/cheer-children-s-healtheducation-economic-resource-imagine-a-community-where-children-s-health-andeducation- records-are-integrated-and-readily-accessible-for-those-who-can-best-helpchildren.

Budde, R. (1988). *Education by charter. Key to long-term continuing improvement in American education*. Waltham, MA: Regional Educational Laboratory for

Educational Improvement of the Northeast & Islands. Retrieved from https://www.edreform.com/wp-content/uploads/2014/12/Education-by-Charter-Restructuring-School-Districts-Ray-Budde.pdf.

DeArmond, M., Gill, S., Gross, B., Heyward, G., Lake, R., McKittrick, L., Opalka, A., Pillow, T., Sharma, R., Tuchman, S., Rhim, L., Lancet, S., & Kothari, S. (2019). *Seizing the opportunity: Educating students with disabilities in charter schools.* Retrieved from https://www.crpe.org/sites/default/files/seizing_the_opportunity_10.2019_final.pdf.

IDOE Compass. (2020). https://inview.doe.in.gov/networks/2000000340.

News at IU: Law and Policy (2019, January 23). Research reveals positive trend for students attending mayor-sponsored charter schools. Retrieved from https://news.iu.edu/stories/2019/01/iupui/releases/23-positive-trend-students-attending-mayor-sponsored-charter-schools-research.html.

Rattermann, M., Angelov, A. D., Reddicks, T., & Monk, J. (2019, June). The Paramount Health Data Project: How school nurse encounter data can improve academic success. National School Based Health Alliance Conference. Washington, DC.

Rattermann, M. J., Angelov, A. D., Reddicks, T., & Monk, J. (2021). Advancing health equity by addressing social determinants of health: Using health data to improve educational outcomes. *PLOS-One*.

Reddicks, T. (2018). Keynote Session. Indiana School Nurses Association Conference. Indianapolis, IN.

Reddicks, T., & Monk, J. (2019, December). Using health data to improve academic outcomes. 20th Annual National Blue Ribbon Schools of Excellence Conference. Orlando, FL.

Reddicks, T., Monk, J., Rattermann, M., & Angelov, A. D. (2018, June). Paramount Brookside: A national site visit. National School Based Health Care Conference. Indianapolis, IN.

Chapter 3

A Schoolwide Approach to Health Care

An Urban School's Journey

Shy-Quon Ely II and Nadia Miller

In the wake of the COVID-19 pandemic, schools across the country are rethinking how they implement school-based health services and the role they play moving forward. One urban elementary school chose to take a reflective data-driven approach to understanding their students and combating COVID learning loss. This chapter shares the types of data they collected and how they used those data to inform their instructional practices for students. Specifically, this chapter sheds light on the academic impact of visiting the school nurse's office for medication administration.

THE SCHOLAR SCHOOL

The mission of the Scholar School (TSS) is to provide the community with an accelerated learning institution that propels scholars academically by utilizing a holistic curriculum built upon community engagement, project-based learning and the leading literacy, socioemotional, and neuroscientific research, thus providing scholars rich opportunities for enrichment, achievement, and increasing degrees of impact in every field of endeavor.

TSS was founded in 2016 with its first academic year in 2017–2018. The target population of the school is minority, low-income, at-risk students. The goal of TSS is to "propel scholars academically through an accelerated curriculum that focus on neuroscientific instruction and learning, staff and community collaboration and a holistic emphasis that incorporates physical nutrition and mental wellness." TSS opened in the fall of 2017 with an enrollment of approximately 501 students across grades K–6. TSS's enrollment for the

2018–2019 school year stood at approximately 534 students, with a student population of 83 percent African American, 11 percent Hispanic, 3 percent White, and 7 percent multiracial. TSS has maintained the diversity from its opening semester as is reflected in the data used in this chapter.

TSS provides students with a standards-based education aligned with the Indiana Academic Standards. TSS uses the ReadyGen curriculum for language arts and Eureka Math for mathematics. TSS also provide the Historic Journey curriculum, which is currently being integrated into the social studies and history curriculums. TSS employs a mastery-based model of instruction, using student assessment data to determine when a student has demonstrated a deep level of understanding of the content of an educational standard before progressing to the next standard. Because of the implementation of the mastery-based model, TSS relies heavily on data-driven instructional practices and high-quality student assessments.

TSS has been collecting both student health data, in the form of visits to the school nurse, and academic assessment data, in the form of the Northwest Evaluation Association Measures of Academic Progress (NWEA MAP) since the school opened to students in the 2017–2018 academic year. This longitudinal dataset forms the basis of the following report. The report will examine overall student health through an analysis of the type and quantity of visits to the school nurse, while academic success will be examined through an analysis of student growth on the NWEA MAP, as well as a comparison of Ignite Achievement Academy student progress to a virtual control group provided by NWEA. This control group is made up of students matched to Ignite students for grade, ethnicity, gender, and fall scores on the NWEA MAP. Their growth over an academic year will be compared to that of TSS students' growth over the same academic year. Both the student health data and the academic assessment data will be disaggregated by student grade, gender, ethnicity, and special education and English as a new language (ENL) status.

The Dataset

The student health data used in this report is from the 2017–2018 school year through to the end of the 2021–2022 school year. The dataset is made up of 14,739 health care visits (HCV) to the school nurse's office from 1,160 individual students. The longitudinal nature of this dataset means that an individual student can contribute data over multiple academic years; consequently there are 1,833 "HCV students"—or students who contributed data in each academic year—and only 1,160 unique students who contributed data to the overall dataset. The breakdown of HCVs by academic year can be seen in table 3.1. The total number of students was calculated using the number of individual students assessed each year using the NWEA MAP and includes students who did not visit the school nurse over the course of the academic year ("non-HCV students"). Because not all students visited the school nurse but all TSS students were assessed with the NWEA MAP, the use of the number of students assessed with the NWEA MAP provides a more accurate estimate of the overall number of students per year. Finally, it is important to note that COVID-19 protocols began in the spring semester of the 2019–2020 academic year (as signified by *) and continued into the 2020–2021 academic year.

To provide a clear view of the distribution of HCVs across relevant subcategories, the data was also disaggregated according to grade level (table 3.2 and table 3.3), gender (figure 3.2 and figure 3.3), ethnicity (figure 3.3), special education status (figure 3.1), status as an English learner (table 3.4), and free/reduced lunch status (table 3.5). When viewing the disaggregated data in the tables to follow, it is important to note that the dataset is very large and there are instances where a specific students' data will be incomplete. Demographic data, such as grade, gender, and ethnicity, were not available for all of students in the dataset. Consequently, across tables the total number of students with HCVs will not always total to the 1,833 HCV students seen in table 3.1, or the 1,160 unique students referenced earlier.

As can be seen in table 3.1, while both the total number of students with and without HCVs varied from year to year, the percentage of students who came to the school nurse remained stable for the two years prior to the onset of COVID-19, increased during the first of the pandemic, and then decreased substantially after, before returning to higher than prepandemic levels. A more complete set of analyses examining the impact of COVID-19 on the number and type of HCVs will be presented in a later section of this chapter.

When the overall number of HCV is disaggregated by grade, as seen in table 3.2, the overall pattern of the data suggests that use of the school nurse was consistent across grades, with both the percentage of students

Table 3.1. Total HCVs by Academic Year

School Year	# of HCV Students	% of All HCV Students	Total Number of HCV	% of Students with HCV	Average HCV per Student	Total # of Students
2017–18	443	24%	4,825	66%	10.9	675
2018–19	471	26%	3,460	68%	7.3	709
2019–20*	321	17%	1,659	81%	5.2	408
2020–21	262	15%	1,495	58%	5.7	454
2021–22	336	18%	3,300	76%	9.8	446
Total	**1,833**	**100%**	**14,739**	**71%**	**7.8**	**2,692**

*2019–2020 data collected and impacted by COVID.

Table 3.2. Total HCVs by Grade Level

Grade	# of HCV Students	% of HCV Students	# of HCV	% of HCV
K	272	15%	1,742	12%
1	330	18%	2,760	19%
2	335	19%	2,512	17%
3	309	17%	2,063	14%
4	265	15%	2,262	15%
5	207	11%	1,936	13%
6	91	5%	1,464	10%
Total	**1,809**	**100%**	**14,739**	**100%**

with HCVs and the percentage of HCVs roughly equal at each grade level. There was a slight difference between the percentage of HCV students and the percent of HCV visits for sixth-grade students, however, the comparatively small number of students making up this sample (ninety-one) makes this data inconclusive.

When disaggregated by both grade and academic year, as seen in table 3.3, the data again shows that HCVs were evenly distributed across grade levels in each academic year. While the data for any given year might suggest that a particular grade made more or fewer HCVs, there was no consistent difference between grades that appeared across the academic years.

When the HCV data is disaggregated by the students' special education status there is a consistent difference between the percentage of special education students in the overall population of HCV students and their usage of the school nurse's office, with the special education students having significantly more HCVs than would be predicted based on their representation in the overall sample. The overall difference is substantial, with special education students comprising 17 percent of the overall sample but responsible for 32 percent of the HCVs—a difference of 15 percent. (The HCV data disaggregated by special education status can be seen in table 3.4.)

This pattern was consistent across each of the academic years, with the data from the 2021–2022 school year revealing a difference of 24 percent between special education students' representation in the sample (14 percent) and the percentage of HCVs (38 percent). The consistency of this finding across academic years and the overall size of the sample (1,523 general education students and 310 special education students) provides confidence that this pattern is one that would replicate across samples. Because the NWEA MAP data did not include information regarding students' special education status, it was not possible to provide data regarding the percentages of each designation in the overall Ignite Achievement Academy student population.

Table 3.3. Total HCVs by Academic Year and Grade

School Year	Grade	# of HCV Students	% of HCV Students	# of HCV	% of HCV
2017–18	K	79	18%	888	18%
	1	78	18%	710	15%
	2	106	24%	1,046	22%
	3	68	15%	457	9%
	4	51	12%	620	13%
	5	47	10%	675	14%
	6	14	3%	429	9%
	Total	443	100%	4,825	100%
2018–19	K	82	17%	429	12%
	1	85	18%	831	24%
	2	85	18%	503	15%
	3	89	19%	597	17%
	4	68	14%	482	14%
	5	46	10%	268	8%
	6	16	4%	350	10%
	Total	471	100%	3,460	100%
2019–20*	K	43	13%	133	8%
	1	70	22%	350	21%
	2	58	18%	361	22%
	3	68	21%	300	18%
	4	49	16%	394	24%
	5	23	7%	94	6%
	6	10	3%	27	2%
	Total	321	100%	1,659	100%
2020–21	K	38	14%	94	6%
	1	52	20%	410	27%
	2	49	19%	153	10%
	3	37	14%	364	24%
	4	48	18%	245	16%
	5	36	14%	226	15%
	6	2	1%	3	0%
	Total	262	100%	1,495	100%
2021–22	K	33	9%	198	6%
	1	56	16%	459	14%
	2	41	12%	449	14%
	3	52	16%	345	10%
	4	49	15%	521	16%
	5	56	17%	673	20%
	6	49	15%	655	20%
	Total	336	100%	3,300	100%

*2019–2020 data collected and impacted by COVID.

Table 3.4. HCVs by Student

School Year	SPED Status	# of HCV Students	% of HCV Students	# of HCV	% of HCV
2017–18	General Education	365	82%	3,135	65%
	Special Education	78	18%	1,690	35%
2018–19	General Education	388	82%	2,271	66%
	Special Education	83	18%	1,189	34%
2019–20*	General Education	261	81%	1,180	71%
	Special Education	60	19%	479	29%
2020–21	General Education	226	86%	927	62%
	Special Education	36	14%	568	38%
2021–22	General Education	283	84%	2,527	77%
	Special Education	53	16%	773	23%
Total	**General Education**	**1,523**	**83%**	**10,040**	**68%**
	Special Education	**310**	**17%**	**4,699**	**32%**

*2019–2020 data collected and impacted by COVID.

The impact of special education status will be examined in more detail in a further section of this report.

SPECIAL EDUCATION AND HCVS

The number of HCVs disaggregated by special education status can be seen in figure 3.1. As in the preceding tables, statistically significant differences between means are denoted by an asterisk and were determined using two-tailed independent sample t-tests with alpha <.05. As can be seen in figure 3.1, special education students account for significantly more medication dosage HCVs than general education students. Significant differences were also found in the "other" category, as well as in psychological/social visits.

Given the prevalence of medications for attention disorders among students diagnosed with ADHD/ADD it is not surprising to see a significant difference in the number of visits to the school nurse for medication administration between special education students, who may have an IEP for their attention disorders, and the general education population. The significant differences between special education and general education students in psychological/social and "other" types of HCVs suggests that students with special needs may be visiting the school nurse more frequently than their peers for reasons that are not always connected to the administration of the medications, or even easily determined physical ailments.

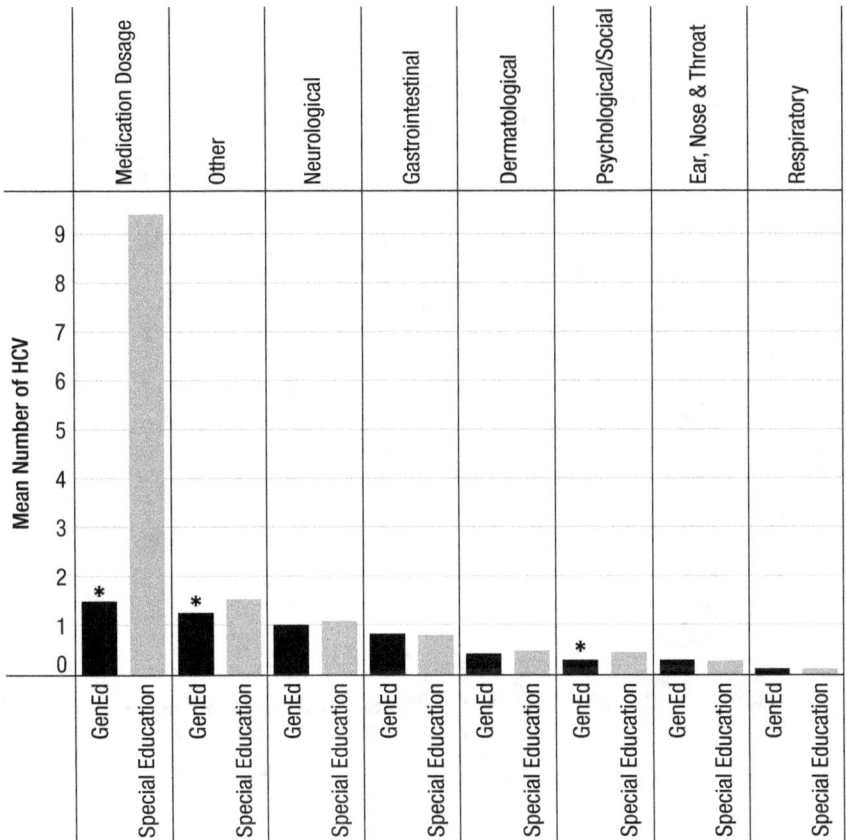

Figure 3.1. Mean Number of HCV Type by Special Education Status

Further examination of the data from students in special education to examine the impact of gender can be seen in figure 3.2, which shows the HCV data disaggregated by special education and gender. As with the examination of overall HCV by gender and ethnicity done previously, the graph is showing stacked means as a way to illustrate the impact of gender and is not an accurate description of the actual mean number of HCV types.

When the data is presented in this way it is easy to see that boys in special education make up a large proportion (mean of 11.42) of the medication dosage visits to the school nurse as compared to girls (mean of 4.02). These figures can also be compared to the students in general education, where the mean number of medication dosage visits for boys is 1.73 and for girls is 1.38. As noted earlier, the fact that students with special needs make up a larger proportion of medication dosage HCVs is not unexpected; boys in special education make up a disproportionate number of these visits.

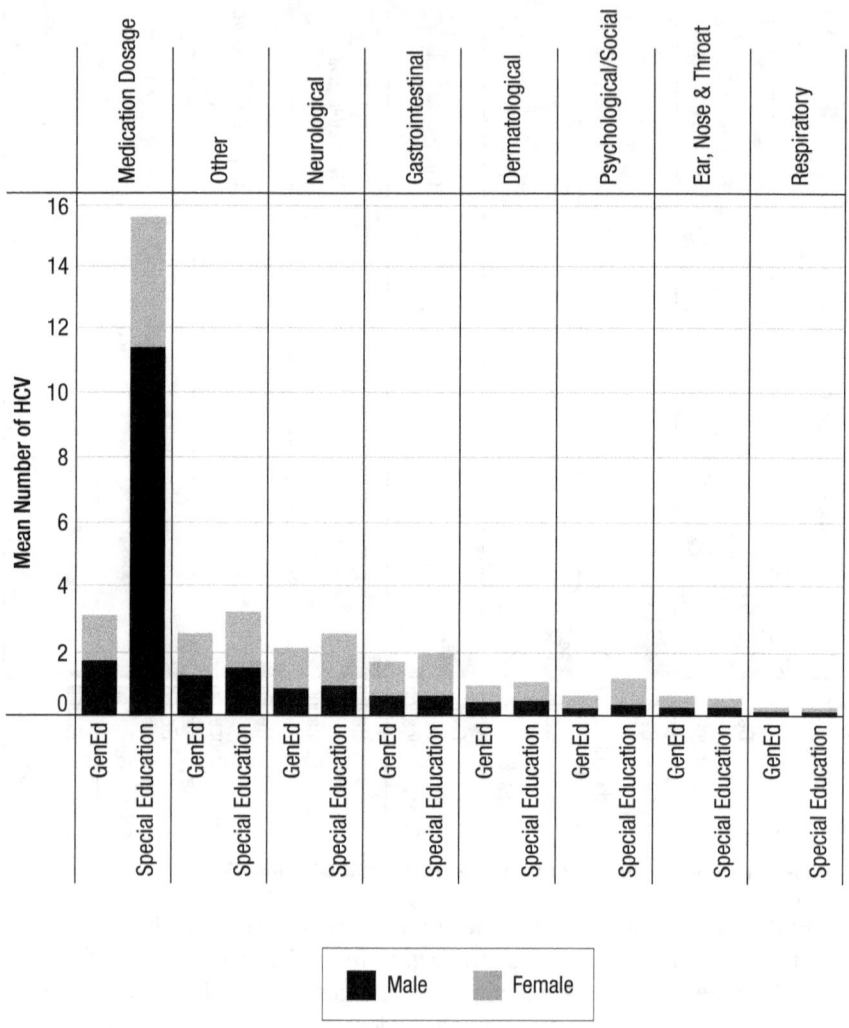

Figure 3.2. Stacked Means for Special Education and Gender

One final disaggregation of the HCV data examines only the medication dosage data and disaggregates along special education status, ethnicity, and gender. This data can be seen in figure 3.3 and shows that African American students are overall more likely to be visiting the school nurse for medication dosage and that African American boys in special education were the most frequent visitors to the school nurse for medication dosage by a considerable margin, with a mean of 13.7 medication dosage visits as compared to African American girls with a mean of 4.13 medication dosage visits and African American boys in general education with a mean of 1.7 medication dosage visits.

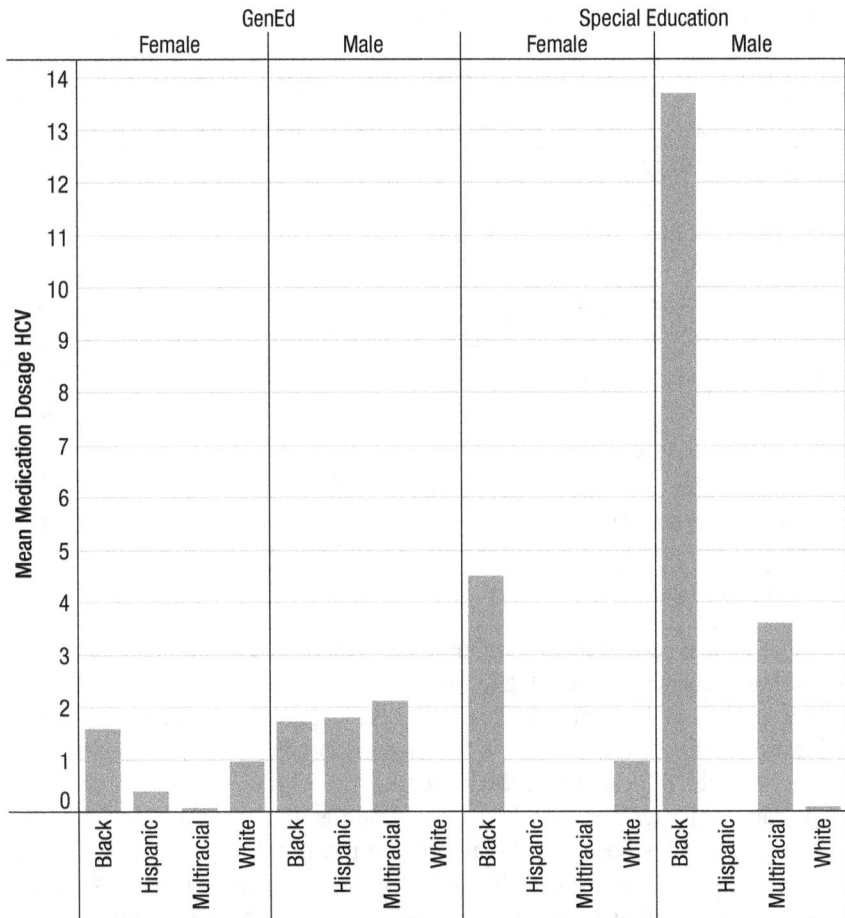

Figure 3.3. Medication Dosage HCV by Special Education Status, Ethnicity, and Gender

NWEA does not include special education, ENL, or free/reduced lunch status in the data files that can be downloaded from their secure website; consequently these designations were imported from the HCV data files. Because not all students who have been assessed using the NWEA MAP have visited the school nurse and thus contributed to the HCV dataset, the analyses of special education, ENL, and free/reduced lunch status will be performed over a subset of the NWEA dataset. Because this is now a truncated dataset, and the number of special education and ENL students is considerably smaller than the general education population, the number of students contributing to each data point will be included in the following table.

As can be seen in table 3.5, special education students make up from 14 percent to 19 percent of the Ignite student population tested with NWEA

Table 3.5. NWEA MAP by Special Education Status

Academic Year		Language Arts		Mathematics	
		General Education	Special Education	General Education	Special Education
2017–18	NWEA Score	172	164	174	167
	N	366	79	368	78
2018–19	NWEA Score	169	164	171	168
	N	405	88	400	91
2019–20*	NWEA Score	169	167	170	172
	N	229	48	230	48
2020–21	NWEA Score	169	168	173	169
	N	284	46	281	46
2021–22	NWEA Score	175	175	178	178
	N	281	46	286	45
Overall Average	**NWEA Score**	**171**	**167**	**173**	**170**
	N	**892**	**152**	**898**	**152**

*2019–2020 data collected and impacted by COVID.

MAP. As noted earlier, this figure may not reflect the actual number of special education students at Ignite due to losing approximately 30 percent of the data when relying on the available data in the HCV database to determine special education status. It is also unwise to draw any conclusions regarding the academic abilities or academic growth of students with special needs given the wide range of cognitive and behavioral abilities this population of students can exhibit. The NWEA MAP may provide useful information regarding the current academic skills of a student with special needs, but it is not designed to assess their overall academic growth and cognitive/behavioral competencies. Because of this limitation and the limitations of the dataset as a whole, any conclusions regarding students in special education and their overall academic abilities or growth must be understood within the COVID context.

CONCLUSION

When the HCV data is disaggregated by the students' special education status there is a consistent difference between the percentage of special education students in the overall population of HCV students and their usage of the school nurse's office, with the special education students having significantly more HCVs than would be predicted based on their representation in the overall sample. The overall difference is substantial, with special education students comprising 17 percent of the overall sample but responsible for 32 percent of the HCVs—a difference of 15 percent. Like the difference in gender, these differences were consistent over the longitudinal sample. A further disaggregation of this data showed that this disproportionate use of the school nurse office for medication dosage is driven by African American boys with special education status, who have a mean number of 11.42 HCV for medication administration as compared to 1.73 for general education boys and 4.02 for African American girls with special education status.

Chapter 4

The Role of Health in Schools

MTSS Approach and Machine Learning Risk Levels

Carolyn Gentle-Genitty, Francis Bowen, Christopher Kearney, Marlin Jackson, and Nathan Lashbrook

Schools are an essential setting for physical and mental health services for many children and adolescents, particularly in areas with food or housing insecurity or fragmented or scarce social services. In fact, in many areas, schools are the de facto primary source for such care. As such, many schools have gravitated toward coordinated, integrated approaches to arranging physical and mental health care for students. These approaches parallel those designed to address multiple individual domains of functioning in students, such as academic performance, and to address complex systemic problems such as school safety, disciplinary issues, and climate (Briesch et al., 2020). Examples of such systems (and domains) include innovative curricula (academic achievement), social-emotional learning and related programs (life skills), teacher and mentor support (violence), classroom management (climate), school-based health centers (physical health), and school counselors, school psychologists, and school-based social workers, including those affiliated with school-based mental health centers (mental health) (for example, Arenson et al., 2019; Corcoran and Edward Thomas, 2021; Reaves et al., 2022).

These coordinated, delivered through simply by being present in school and through integrated systems of support are often arranged in tiers (multitiered systems of support) based on individual student needs that include Tier 1 strategies to help prevent a problem or to augment an area of strength, Tier 2 strategies to provide early intervention to those in need of extra assistance, and Tier 3 strategies to provide later, intensive intervention to those in need of substantial assistance (Stoiber & Gettinger, 2016). Tier 1 strategies are typically more widespread, universal, and preventative in nature; Tier 2 strategies are more circumscribed and targeted to those with acute or emerging problems; and Tier 3 strategies are more intensive and targeted to those with chronic or severe problems. This chapter begins with a general description of Tier 1–based health strategies in schools, followed by discussions of Tier 2 and Tier 3 approaches that can be adapted for students. In addition, these approaches are best distributed when a school can decipher students' level of risk. A machine learning case study, with thirty thousand reported behaviors from one school system, is used to show the feature distributions per target label (low, high, and medium risk). Findings, discussion, and conclusion follow.

TIER 1

School-Based Health Centers

School-based health centers, which can include school-based mental health centers, refer to on-campus facilities where students can receive medical, mental/behavioral, dental, and vision care directly in schools (Arenson et al., 2019). In addition, school-based health centers can be an important part of Tier 1 preventative efforts by working to minimize widespread disease or to help students with chronic or other medical conditions enhance their school attendance and maintain their academic performance (Rice et al., 2020). Preventative efforts can take the form of managing asthma, administering medication, providing vaccinations, mitigating lice outbreaks, and engaging in sexually transmitted disease prevention (for example, Tingey et al., 2021). Related efforts are educational or informative in nature, such as emphasizing the importance of handwashing, oral health care, nutrition, exercise, sleep, and other self-care practices (Love et al., 2019). More specialized efforts can be a part of school-based health centers as well, including information regarding reproductive health, on-campus medical care for pregnant youth in early trimesters, and specialized educational services for students with chronic medical conditions (Marseille et al., 2018).

School-based health centers can also engage in screening services for key issues that can prevent school attendance, often in partnership with hospitals, community-based primary care facilities, and state health departments. In addition, follow up with students who missed school due to illness can be facilitated to ensure a more efficient return to school. In related fashion, on-campus medical care is useful for addressing students with somatic complaints or symptoms in an effort to maintain school attendance for the day (Yoder, 2020). This can require a specific mandate for school nurses to monitor such symptoms and be aware of common strategies to address school attendance problems related to health.

School-based mental health programs are sometimes integrated with school-based health centers but can be a standalone entity as well. These programs are generally designed to promote mental health and to address existing mental health challenges. Much of the focus of these programs has been on substance use prevention to enhance knowledge about the physical effects of alcohol and other drugs as well as insight into personal beliefs about how often peers use drugs, comparing these beliefs to empirical norms (Kolbe, 2019). Other endeavors include interpersonal and coping skills training to facilitate good decision making and establish personal goals with respect to academic and other achievement (O'Connor et al., 2018).

School-based mental health centers also focus on strategies to mitigate the effects of existing psychiatric problems related to possible disruptive, emotional, learning, and other disorders (Sanchez et al., 2018). Examples include coping and interpersonal skills training for stressful school social and academic endeavors, difficult transitions such as divorce, and entry into a new school building; academic and organizational skills for students with developmental, learning, or intellectual disabilities; and conflict resolution, peer mediation, and anger management strategies for students with aggressive interactions (Fenwick-Smith, Dahlberg, & Thompson, 2018). The third may be particularly useful as an alternative to exclusionary disciplinary avenues. School-based mental health centers can also work with caregivers to assist with student behavioral and academic problems and facilitate communication and cooperation with school officials to address such problems in multiple settings (Swick & Powers, 2018). Mental health centers can also help reduce stigma associated with various psychiatric disorders and especially developmental disorders such as autism (Papadopoulos et al., 2019).

School-Based Social-Emotional Learning Programs

Social and emotional learning (SEL) programs are also an important part of school-based Tier 1 initiatives to enhance health in students. These programs focus on social-emotional competencies to mitigate risk for mental disorders and other problems and to develop protective skills for adaptive functioning. Broad skill sets developed in these programs include social, decision making, emotional regulation, and self-awareness skills as well as those related to academic performance and general prosocial behavior (Haymovitz et al., 2018). More specific skill sets relate to self-appraisal, empathy, problem solving, self-care, self-concept, self-improvement, and time management, among others (for example, Voith et al., 2020). Some SEL programs include caregiver and family components as well.

Safety-Oriented Strategies

Tier 1 strategies broadly related to student health also include those designed to increase safety to and within school. The most widespread programs are those aimed to reduce school bullying and violence. Key elements of these programs include clear and enforced rules regarding bullying and violence, conflict resolution, classroom behavior management, contingency plans for emergencies, mentoring and tutoring, peer mediation, support groups, and victim and perpetrator counseling (World Health Organization, 2019). Increased security measures are common to these programs as well to create safe passages to and within schools. Examples include automated lockdowns, barriers, cameras, enhanced police presence, metal detectors, panic buttons, and specially designed doors and windows. Increased supervision by school personnel, particularly in less restricted areas, allows for quicker intervention of conflicts as well.

Safety-oriented strategies intersect as well with those designed to improve school climate and reduce instances of exclusionary discipline. Schoolwide positive behavior support, for example, emphasizes classroom behavior management and academic engagement to augment prosocial behaviors and reduce disruptive behaviors. Key elements include clear expectations and consequences regarding personal responsibility, respect for others, and safety; continuum of consequences based on violation; incentives for prosocial behavior; parent and family involvement; social skills; and universal screening for learning and other problems (Noltemeyer et al., 2019).

Trauma-Informed Practices

School-based trauma-focused practices or trauma-informed teaching/classrooms refer to approaches that consider the impact of trauma on students and integrate knowledge of student trauma into educational and behavioral responses (Stratford et al., 2020). A primary goal is to prevent students who are likely to have experienced adverse events from being retraumatized at school, to provide palliative measures to ease traumatic effects, and to improve educational outcomes for traumatized students (Herrenkohl, Hong, & Verbrugge, 2019). A secondary goal is to identify students who may require more intensive Tier 2/3 services.

A main component of trauma-informed practices is to educate school staff about the signs and effects of trauma and how these can interfere with social and academic performance and be misjudged as behavior in need of disciplinary action (Nadeem et al., 2022). Traumatized youth often have difficulties with emotional regulation, for example, that could interfere with interpersonal and classroom tasks and be viewed as disruptive in nature. Part of trauma-informed practices is to ensure that an emphasis is placed on developing competencies and enhancing a sense of safety for students and to deemphasize deficit narratives and practices that could retraumatize a student (Chafouleas et al., 2016).

Other key components of trauma-informed practices involve classroom management techniques designed to defuse or deescalate potentially volatile situations (Darnell et al., 2019). Teachers, for example, are asked to develop trust-based and collaborative relationships with students with an emphasis on active listening, empathy, multiple forms of communication, and positive affirmations. Teachers are also asked to provide rationales and transparency for expected behavior, extended compliance times for students, and supportive feedback during classroom routines that should be as predictable and consistent as possible. Trauma-informed practices also incorporate strategies to allow students to calm themselves via cooldown areas, dimmed lights, flexible seating, and play and walks as needed (Minahan, 2019).

Antibullying Strategies

Another school-based health initiative has been to reduce bullying and other forms of interpersonal violence on and off (cyber)campus. Main components of antibullying programs include increased supervision of students by staff at school, clear and enforced antibullying policies and consequences, effective classroom behavior management, teacher training, parental involvement, encouraging bystanders to report, direct counseling work with perpetrators and victims, and curriculum-based information regarding socioemotional skills, effects of bullying, and mental health (Gaffney, Ttofi, & Farrington, 2021). Other interventions are targeted more toward the cyberenvironment and include information and communication technologies such as gaming, online counseling, website information, and virtual reality (Nocentini, Zambuto, & Menesini, 2015). Antibullying programs are moderately effective though the specific mechanism of these effects remains unclear (Gaffney, Ttofi, & Farrington, 2019).

TIER 2

Mental Health

Various mental health interventions have been designed to be incorporated into school settings as Tier 2 strategies. These interventions may be more general to address emotional distress or adjustment problems but have also been crafted to address more specific issues. General interventions include components of cognitive behavioral and family therapies to help students manage or mitigate difficult emotions and physical symptoms, problematic thought processes, avoidance, substance use, school disengagement, and comorbid problems (O'Reilly et al., 2018). General interventions can be conducted at school, home, or via telehealth practices by school-based personnel and/or in conjunction with community-based mental health professionals (Soneson et al., 2020).

These interventions can be associated with more intense trauma-focused practices as well. Several treatment packages have been designed for school settings (for example, trauma-focused cognitive behavior therapy, Cohen & Mannarino, 2015; cognitive behavioral intervention for trauma in schools, Jaycox et al., 2012; grief and trauma intervention for children, Salloum & Overstreet, 2012; multimodal trauma treatment, Amaya-Jackson et al., 2003). These packages center on helping students understand trauma, manage anger and grief, regulate emotions, utilize coping and social problem-solving skills, and engage in emotional processing of traumatic events. Caregivers can be involved as well to establish safety plans and help boost resilience in their children (Fondren et al., 2020).

Other Tier 2 mental health initiatives are also geared for specific kinds of problems and contain specially targeted techniques. Examples include Tier 2 practices for students with depression (including suicide prevention and mindfulness; Arora et al., 2019); anxiety (including somatic control exercises and modeling; Sulkowski, Joyce, & Storch, 2012); substance use (including parental monitoring and family-based relations; Van Ryzin et al., 2016); and disruptive behavior (including peer-assisted learning and academic support; Sinclair, Gesel, & Lemons, 2019). Other Tier 2 initiatives are supplemented as well with accommodation plans, extended school counselor sessions, mentoring (see next), and arrangements for safer transportation to and from school (McInerney & McKlindon, 2014). These procedures can be conducted within schools but are often done in conjunction with community-based professionals given that many schools do not have a school counselor (US Department of Education, 2016).

Mentoring

Students with difficulty adjusting to social and academic demands at school may benefit from mentoring programs designed to provide support and to enhance problem-solving capabilities. Various programs have been crafted that focus on peer, teacher, school official, or community member mentors who serve as guides for students at Tier 2. The Check and Connect or Check-in/Check-out program, for example, includes daily meetings with a mentor, regular teacher-parent communication about student academic performance and behavior, and efforts to draw parents into the school setting (Christenson et al., 1999; Miller et al., 2015). Mentors work with students on various skills to manage daily life, including academic, conflict resolution, interpersonal, problem solving, coping, and self-regulation skills. Challenges with peers, family members, and teachers are also addressed in addition to helping students manage stressful transitions and obstacles to school attendance and peer relationships. Mentoring strategies have variable effectiveness in part because standard protocols and specific treatment constructs are often not elucidated clearly (McQuillin et al., 2020).

Physical Health

Tier 2 practices for students with emerging physical health problems have been increasingly important in the pandemic era and typically involve expansion of the mandate given to school nurses and school-based health centers (for example, screening, vaccination). These practices can include working with students and their families who must remain home due to a physical illness as well as students who return to school following a long absence. These practices may be most important for vulnerable students whose main source of health care is at school (Phelps & Sperry, 2020). Management of respiratory conditions often related to school absence, such as asthma, is a key part of Tier 2 services as well (Martin & Sorensen, 2020).

TIER 3

Tier 3 services are designed for students with severe or chronic conditions related to physical or mental health. Crisis management is a key element of these services and initially involves ensuring the physical safety of a student and assessing for psychological trauma (Lai et al., 2016). Additional techniques include normalizing expected reactions to the traumatic event, engaging in empathetic listening, encouraging self-care, identifying sources of assistance, coping strategies to manage reactions, boosting social support, and creating safety plans (Kramer & Landolt, 2011). Both school-based personnel known to a child as well as community-based professionals are typically involved in these situations (Capurso, De Stasio, & Ragni, 2022).

Circumstances such as child maltreatment also carry special mandates such as legal obligations to report.

Other Tier 3 initiatives tend to be broader in scope and include full service community schools, alternative educational pathways, and more personalized instruction to help students navigate an extended crisis or disability that substantially interferes with daily life functioning (for example, Walkington & Bernacki, 2020). Tier 3 cases typically demand close collaboration with physicians, mental health professionals, social services agencies, and legal and developmental professionals to manage complex and longstanding cases (Santiago, Raviv, & Jaycox, 2018). In addition, Tier 3 cases will require creative strategies to help students complete school outside of typical district/academic requirements (Kearney, 2016).

MACHINE LEARNING CASE STUDY

Methods

Machine learning generally combines supervised and unsupervised learning to uncover relationships between and among features with the aim to predict one or more target variables. For instance, with supervised learning, one may have a data point associating the square footage, age, and number of bedrooms to the selling price of a house. Given a sufficient number of historical records, associating square footage, age, and the number of bedrooms to the selling price of a house, the proportions of each feature (square footage, age, and number of bedrooms) are computed to minimize an error metric over all records used to train the model.

A feature of the output of machine learning is classifiers. Classifiers are models that also relate features to a target. In this case, the estimated target is a categorical variable with a finite set of values. The target variable's values are commonly referred to as *classes or labels*. For instance, given the set of real estate data, a classifier model might be used to predict if the square footage, age, and number of bedrooms represents a mobile home, apartment, or a house. In this example, the input into the model are numeric features, and the target represents one of the three class labels: mobile home, apartment, or house. Using a distance metric, typically the Euclidean distance, similarity between multidimensioned data points where each dimension is a separate feature was assessed.

Model

We offer the model herein as a way to leverage reported student behavior data, coupled with trained unsupervised models and supervised models to yield a process for identifying low-, medium-, and high-risk students. Such a system is proposed (Bowen et al., 2022), where K-means clustering is used to identify an initial grouping of students at the classroom level, based on the distribution of their reported behaviors, using the target classes defined in the Building Dreams Platform from the Fight for Life Foundation's innovative service. Clustering is performed to identify the initial three classifications of low-, medium-, and high-risk students. As a behavior is observed—positive or negative—it is logged in the system. The dataset can thereby be aggregated on a per student basis, where each student represents a data point, characterized by the distribution of their total reports.

By assigning class labels to each student, we can perform common descriptive analytics to develop an understanding between low-, medium-, and high-risk students.

Findings

In one case study, the student classification system was trained on approximately thirty thousand reported behaviors for over three hundred K–6 students, then applied to an additional thirty thousand data points in a subsequent academic term.

When evaluating the effectiveness of the clustering algorithm, we can visualize clusters as shown figure 4.1. Each student is characterized using a distribution of five features, representing the type of behavior reported in the Building Dreams Platform. Each of the five features is visualized with each other, to produce the set of 2D graphs, showing the individual clusters. This provides a graphic representation of the cluster separation and allows us to determine the most important features that differentiate the clusters.

When evaluating the classification system, repeatability is critical. We found the proposed system consistent when applied to a subsequent term with thirty thousand reported behaviors. The student population by race and age are given in figures 4.2 and 4.3. Applying the classification system, along with demographic information, we get a clear understanding of demographics relative to determined risk level, as illustrated in figures 4.4 through 4.8.

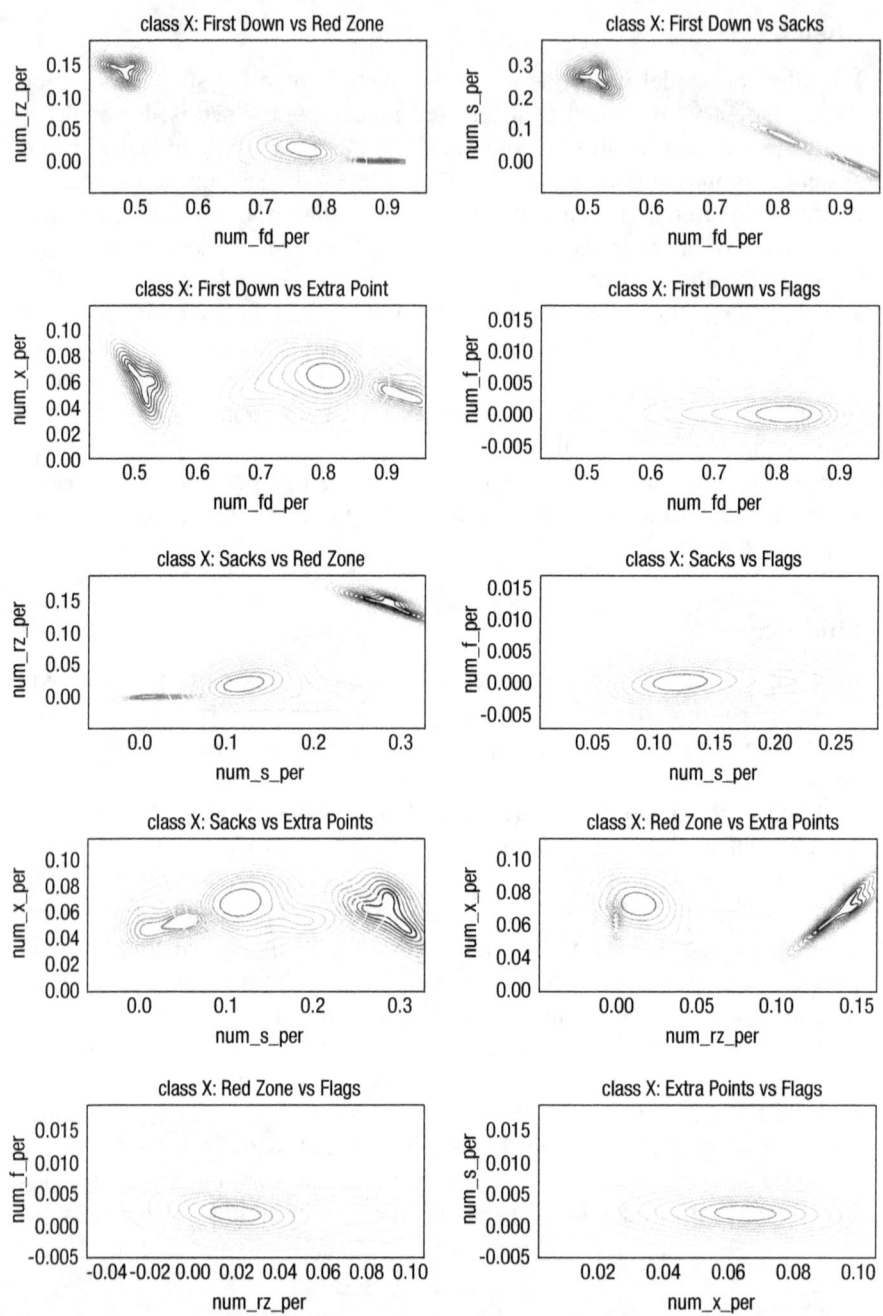

Figure 4.1. Clustering Results, Illustrating the Separation of Features Characterizing Each Student

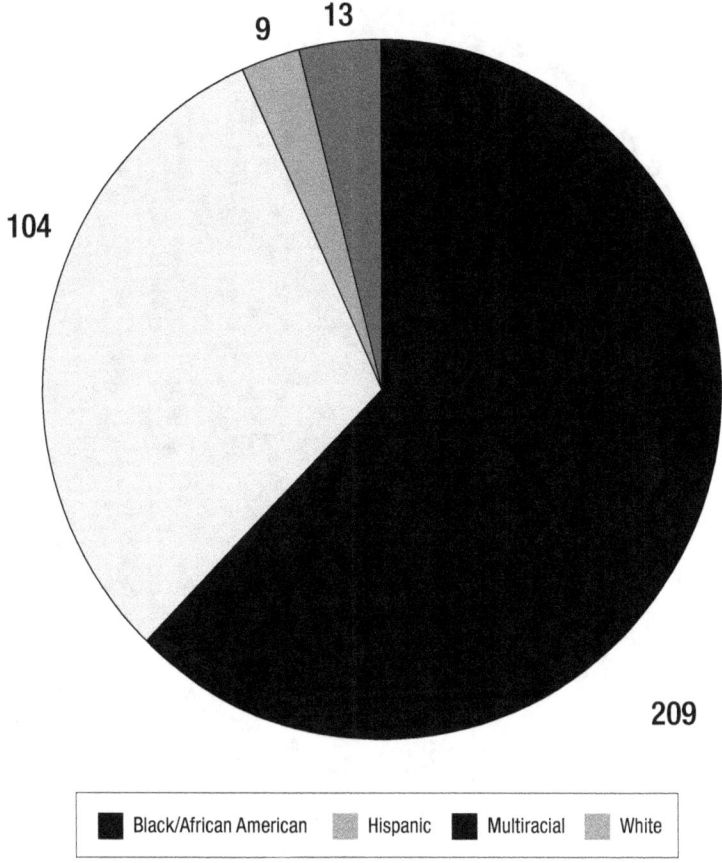

Figure 4.2. Number of Students by Race

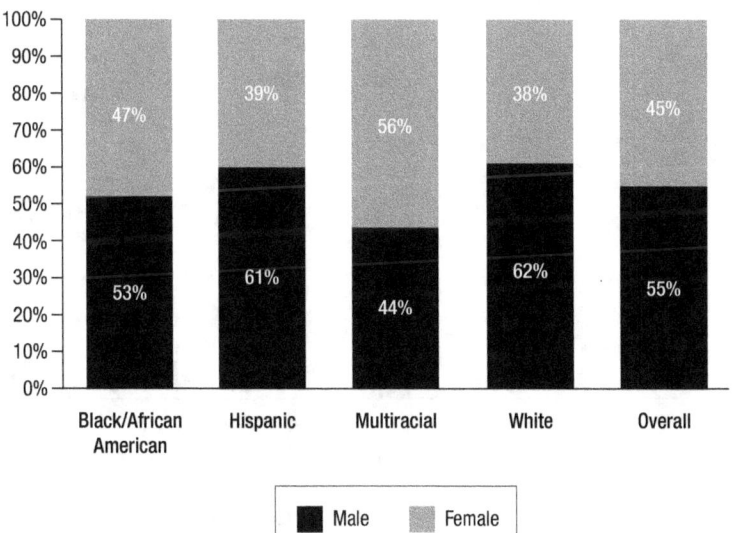

Figure 4.3. Gender Distribution by Race

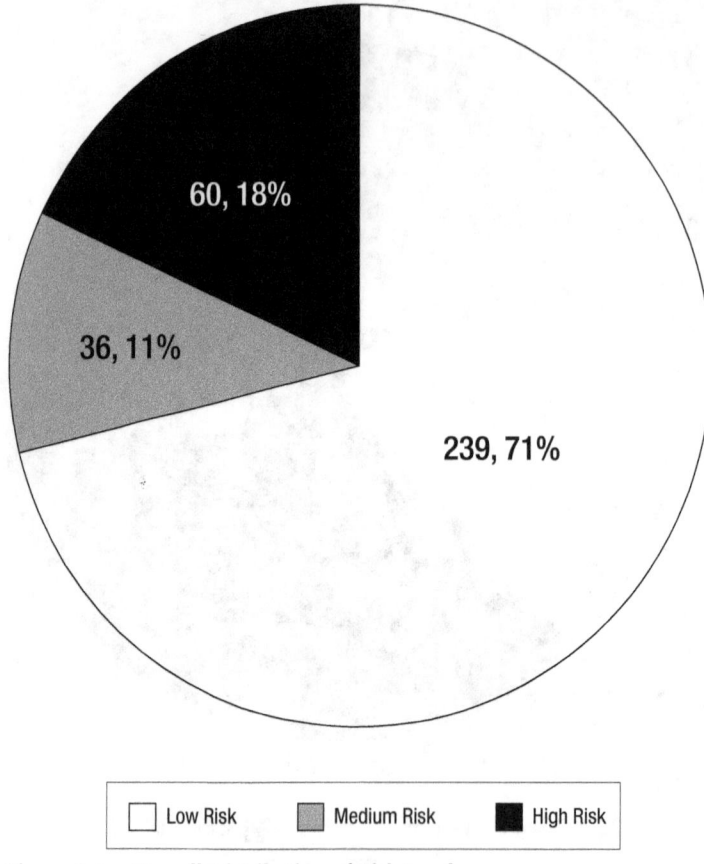

Figure 4.4. Overall Distribution of Risk Level

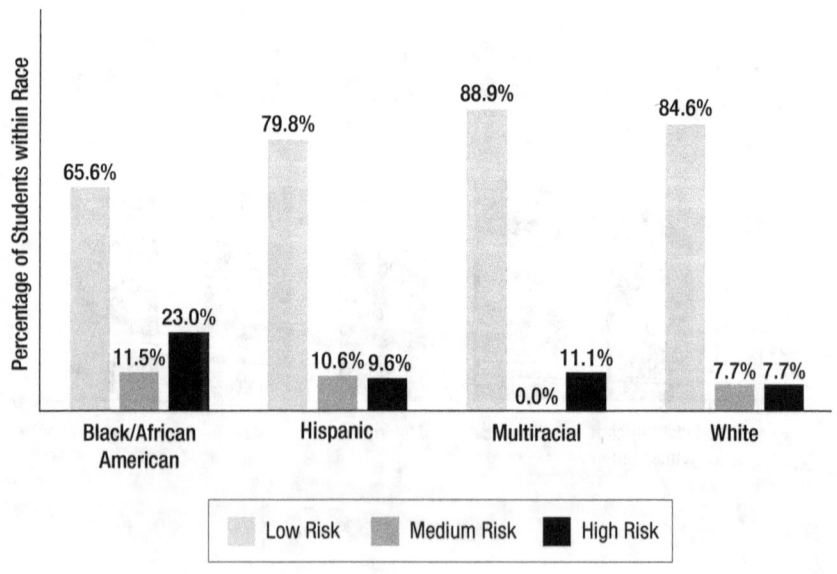

Figure 4.5. Distribution of Risk by Race

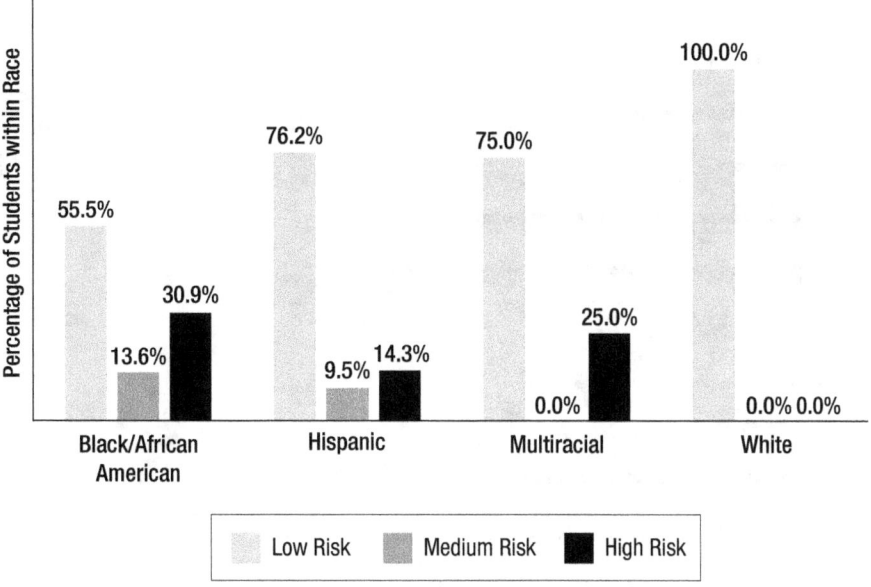

Figure 4.6. Distribution of Risk Level per Race by Males

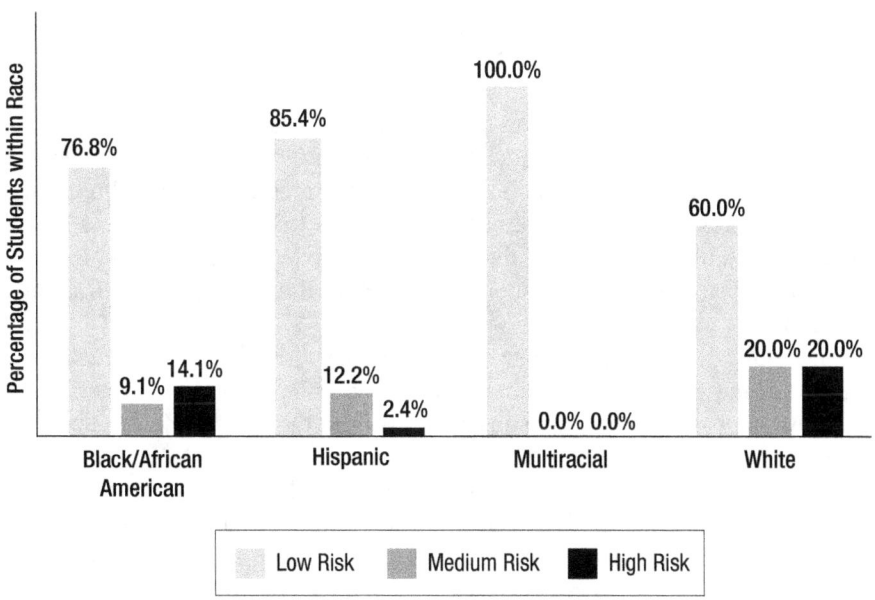

Figure 4.7. Distribution of Risk Level per Race by Females

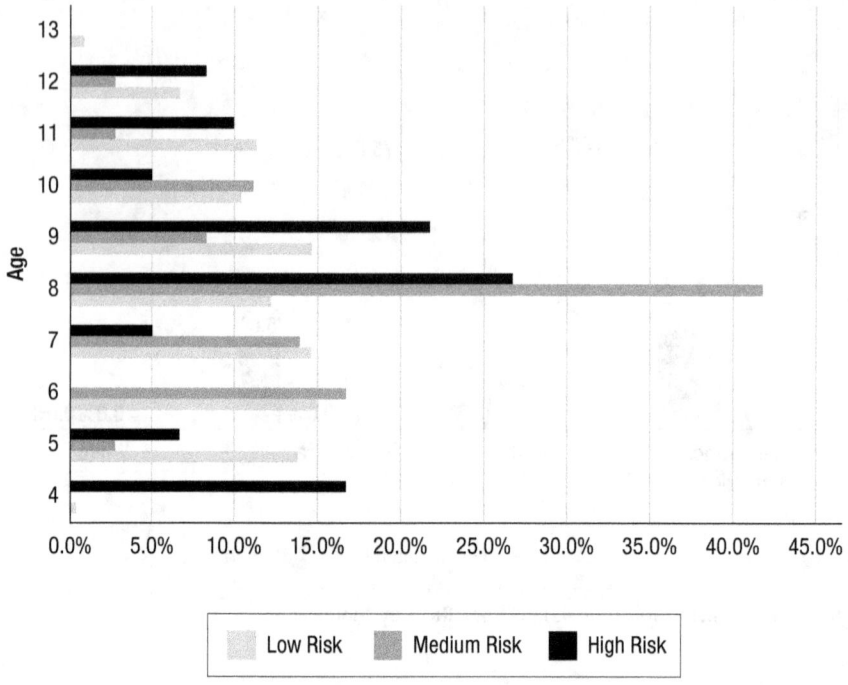

Figure 4.8. Overall Distribution of Risk by Age

DISCUSSION

In the end, what we observed was that no matter the distribution of race, age, or gender, most students (80 percent) presented minimal risk and ultimately may benefit from Tier 1 interventions just by being present in school. Promoting school presence and engagement, with access to universal services and supports, will ultimately impact the health of all students. Being absent is too risky on their academic health, social-emotional health, peer and socialization development, and success.

The application of the machine learning models brings to light interesting insights about the student population in need of support at Tier 2 interventions. Most notably the top five observations from the dataset showed that

1. one in five K–6 students are classified as high risk,
2. just about one-third of this student population exhibit concerning behaviors,
3. one in five of those who were African American were also labeled as male and high risk,

4. males accounted for a significant number of negatively reported behaviors in other races too but not for white students, and
5. white girls were disproportionately represented in the high-risk category.

In lieu of these findings school administrators, personnel, and educators should provide Tier 2 and 3 that are culturally relevant to the student populations most at risk with special considerations for programming that is gender specific.

For Tier 3 interventions, it was more about scaling intensity of Tier 2 approaches. It was observed from the reported data—positive and negative reasons—attendance and attendance-related reasons were the differentiating factor between students falling into the low- or high-risk group. See the summary in table 4.1. For instance, the low-risk group, those who were present, engaged, and ready to learn, can be characterized as those students who follow rules, contribute to class discussions, and report to class on time. When compared to the high-risk group, those who were mostly absent, not engaged, or available to learn, those students did not follow directions, violated rules, and were out for fights or violent actions. They differ by a factor of 2 and 3, respectively, and showed a stark difference between clusters. However both low- and high-risk student behavior correlated to school attendance and engagement.

Within the Building Dreams Platform, each reported reason can be mapped back to a core value. As such, core values are tracked for both positively and negatively tracked behavior. When mapping the risk groups back to the core values, we observe that the clear differentiating factors between low- and high-risk groups are *core values directly related to peer relationships*. More specifically, positive relationships, respect for physical settings, and respect

Table 4.1. Specific Reported Reasons Differentiating Low- and High-Risk Students

Reason	Risk		
	Low	Medium	High
Follows school rules	9.81%	6.39%	3.34%
Contributed to class discussion	7.74%	4.28%	3.30%
Reported to class on time	6.10%	3.46%	2.07%
Follows directions on the first time	9.57%	15.01%	13.67%
Turned in assignment/homework	3.02%	4.36%	1.52%
Showed consistent work ethic	10.30%	12.54%	11.41%
Did not follow directions	0.36%	2.99%	10.03%
Violated rule	0.02%	0.24%	2.51%
Fighting/violent actions	0.01%	0.66%	2.26%

Note: Table depicts only top three reported reasons per class label relative to other two classes.

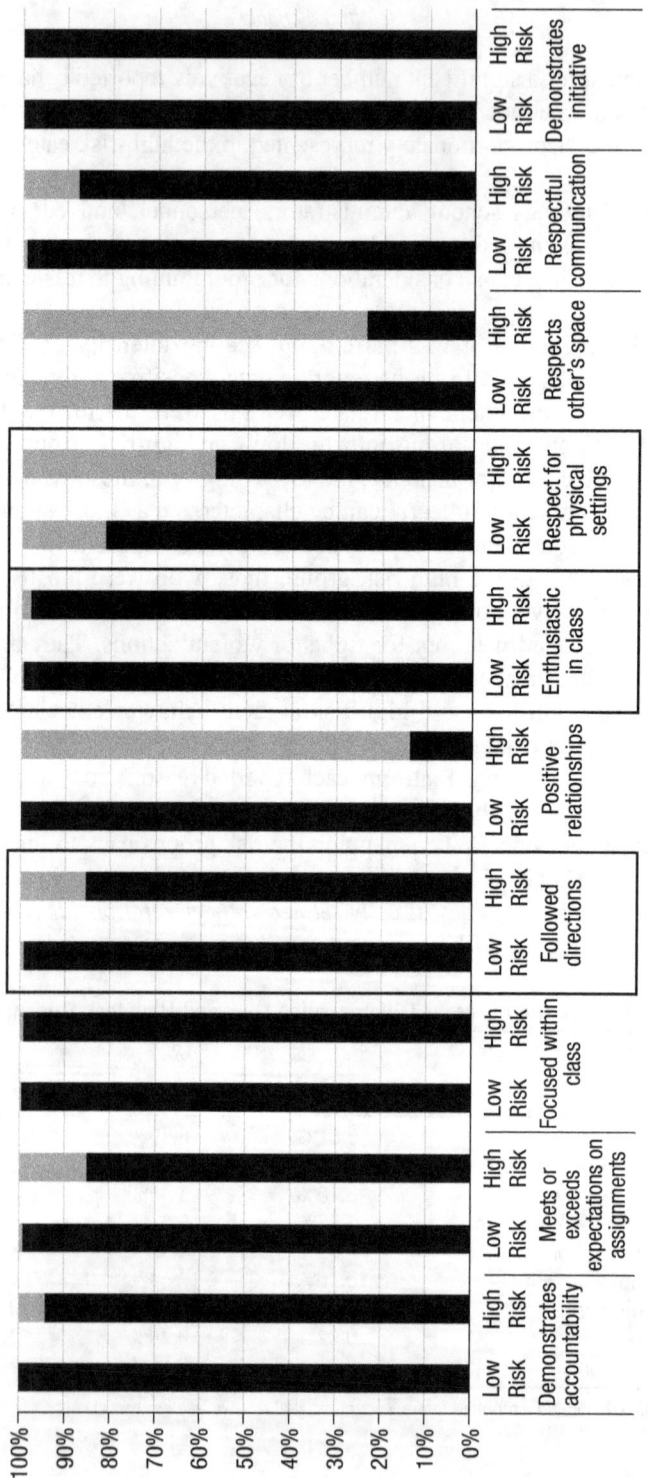

Figure 4.9. Core Values by Risk Classification

for other's spaces are shown to be key differentiators. By examining the proportion of positive reports to negative reports, we find that positive relationships for the low-risk group were always reported positive, while the near inverse is true for the high-risk group, as highlighted in figure 4.9.

Thereby it behooves us to conclude that positive relationships are also integral to health outcomes in schools for all students regardless of risk levels. One consistent observation, agnostic of race, is the larger concentration of medium- and high-risk students between the ages of seven and nine. Health in schools is predicated on access to services and resources and most of them should be universal to all students enabling the building of positive relationships. Programming specific by gender and age is also a must particularly for Tier 2 approaches. The tiered approaches help us organize and better share scarce resources especially in schools with limited resources. Figure 4.1 provides evidence that common machine learning techniques are effective when employed in an academic environment. It should be noted that the success of machine learning models, regardless of application, are dependent on the quality and quantity of the data. Proper infrastructure must be in place to collect and curate data that is correlated to a target. Moreover, sufficient security must be considered when considering the sensitive nature of academic data. The overall classification of students, from a pure data-driven lens, is most useful when other external data is available. Modeling the absences and academic performance can be strengthened through collaboration and data sharing with the schools. Moreover, this type of analysis can easily be extrapolated using other forms of data, such as school health records.

REFERENCES

Amaya-Jackson, L., Reynolds, V., Murray, M. C., McCarthy, G., Nelson, A., Cherney, M. S., . . . & March, J. S. (2003). Cognitive-behavioral treatment for pediatric posttraumatic stress disorder: Protocol and application in school and community settings. *Cognitive and Behavioral Practice, 10*, 204–13. https://doi.org/10.1016/S1077-7229(03)80032-9.

Arenson, M., Hudson, P. J., Lee, N., & Lai, B. (2019). The evidence on school-based health centers: A review. *Global Pediatric Health, 6*, 2333794X19828745. https://doi.org/10.1177/2333794X19828745.

Arora, P. G., Collins, T. A., Dart, E. H., Hernández, S., Fetterman, H., & Doll, B. (2019). Multi-tiered systems of support for school-based mental health: A systematic review of depression interventions. *School Mental Health, 11*, 240–64. https://doi.org/10.1007/s12310-019-09314-4.

Bowen, F., Lashbrook, N., Siegler, Gentle-Genitty, C., Jackson, M., & Mitchell. (2022). https://fightforlifefoundation.org/building-dreams-case-study/.

Briesch, A. M., Chafouleas, S. M., Nissen, K., and Long, S. (2020). A review of state-level procedural guidance for implementing multitiered systems of support for behavior (MTSS-B). *Journal of Positive Behavioral Interventions, 22*, 131–44. https://doi.org/10.1177/1098300719884707.

Capurso, M., De Stasio, S., & Ragni, B. (2022). Universal crisis psychoeducational interventions in schools: A scoping review. *School Psychology International*, 01430343221104986. https://doi.org/10.1177/01430343221104986.

Chafouleas, S. M., Johnson, A. H., Overstreet, S., & Santos, N. M. (2016). Toward a blueprint for trauma-informed service delivery in schools. *School Mental Health, 8*, 144–62. 10.1007/s12310-015-9166-8.

Christenson, S. L., Sinclair, M. F., Thurlow, M. L., & Evelo, D. (1999). Promoting student engagement with school using the Check & Connect model. *Journal of Psychologists and Counsellors in Schools, 9*, 169–84. https://doi.org/10.1017/S1037291100003083.

Cohen, J. A., & Mannarino, A. P. (2015). Trauma-focused cognitive behavior therapy for traumatized children and families. *Child and Adolescent Psychiatric Clinics, 24*, 557–70.

Corcoran, T., & Edward Thomas, M. K. (2021). School-wide positive behaviour support as evidence-making interventions. *Research in Education, 111*, 108–25. https://doi.org/10.1177/00345237211034884.

Darnell, T., Hager, K., & Loprinzi, P. D. (2019). The impact of school nurses in Kentucky public high schools. *Journal of School Nursing*, 35(6), 434–41. https://doi.org/10.1177/1059840518785954.

Fenwick-Smith, A., Dahlberg, E. E., & Thompson, S. C. (2018). Systematic review of resilience-enhancing, universal, primary school-based mental health promotion programs. *BMC Psychology, 6*, 1–17. https://doi.org/10.1186/s40359-018-0242-3.

Fondren, K., Lawson, M., Speidel, R., McDonnell, C. G., & Valentino, K. (2020). Buffering the effects of childhood trauma within the school setting: A systematic review of trauma-informed and trauma-responsive interventions among trauma-affected youth. *Children and Youth Services Review, 109*, 104691. https://doi.org/10.1016/j.childyouth.2019.104691.

Gaffney, H., Ttofi, M. M., & Farrington, D. P. (2019). Evaluating the effectiveness of school-bullying prevention programs: An updated meta-analytical review. *Aggression and Violent Behavior, 45*, 111–33. https://doi.org/10.1016/j.avb.2018.07.001.

Gaffney, H., Ttofi, M. M., & Farrington, D. P. (2021). What works in anti-bullying programs? Analysis of effective intervention components. *Journal of School Psychology, 85*, 37–56. https://doi.org/10.1016/j.jsp.2020.12.002.

Haymovitz, E., Houseal-Allport, P., Lee, R. S., & Svistova, J. (2018). Exploring the perceived benefits and limitations of a school-based social–emotional learning program: A concept map evaluation. *Children & Schools, 40*, 45–54. https://doi.org/10.1093/cs/cdx029.

Herrenkohl, T. I., Hong, S., & Verbrugge, B. (2019). Trauma-informed programs based in schools: Linking concepts to practices and assessing the evidence. *American Journal of Community Psychology, 64*, 373–88. https://doi.org/10.1002/ajcp.12362.

Jaycox, L. H., Kataoka, S. H., Stein, B. D., Langley, A. K., & Wong, M. (2012). Cognitive behavioral intervention for trauma in schools. *Journal of Applied School Psychology, 28*, 239–55.

Kearney, C. A. (2016). *Managing school absenteeism at multiple tiers: An evidence-based and practical guide for professionals.* New York: Oxford University Press.

Kolbe, L. J. (2019). School health as a strategy to improve both public health and education. *Annual Review of Public Health, 40*, 443–63. https://doi.org/10.1146/annurev-publhealth-040218-043727.

Kramer, D. N., & Landolt, M. A. (2011). Characteristics and efficacy of early psychological interventions in children and adolescents after single trauma: A meta-analysis. *European Journal of Psychotraumatology, 2*, 7858. https://doi.org/10.3402/ejpt.v2i0.7858.

Lai, C. K., Skinner, A. L., Cooley, E., Murrar, S., Brauer, M., Devos, T., Calanchini, J., Xiao, Y. J., Pedram, C., Marshburn, C. K., Simon, S., Blanchar, J. C., Joy-Gaba, J. A., Conway, J., Redford, L., Klein, R. A., Roussos, G., Schellhaas, F. M. H., Burns, M., ... Nosek, B. A. (2016). Reducing implicit racial preferences: II. Intervention effectiveness across time. *Journal of Experimental Psychology: General, 145*(8), 1001–1016. https://doi.org/10.1037/xge0000179.

Love, H. E., Schlitt, J., Soleimanpour, S., Panchal, N., & Behr, C. (2019). Twenty years of school-based health care growth and expansion. *Health Affairs, 38*, 755–64. https://doi.org/10.1377/hlthaff.2018.05472.

Marseille, E., Mirzazadeh, A., Biggs, M. A., Miller, A., Horvath, H., Lightfoot, M., ... & Kahn, J. G. (2018). Effectiveness of school-based teen pregnancy prevention programs in the USA: A systematic review and meta-analysis. *Prevention Science, 19*, 468–89. https://doi.org/10.1007/s11121-017-0861-6.

Martin, E. G., & Sorensen, L. C. (2020). Protecting the health of vulnerable children and adolescents during COVID-19–related K–12 school closures in the US. *JAMA Health Forum, 1*, e200724. https://doi.org/10.1001/jamahealthforum.2020.0724.

McInerney, M., & McKlindon, A. (2014). *Unlocking the door to learning: Trauma-informed classrooms and transformational schools.* Education Law Center.

McQuillin, S. D., Lyons, M. D., Clayton, R. J., & Anderson, J. R. (2020). Assessing the impact of school-based mentoring: Common problems and solutions associated with evaluating nonprescriptive youth development programs. *Applied Developmental Science, 24*, 215–29. https://doi.org/10.1080/10888691.2018.1454837.

Miller, L. M., Dufrene, B. A., Sterling, H. E., Olmi, D. J., & Bachmayer, E. (2015). The effects of check-in/check-out on problem behavior and academic engagement in elementary school students. *Journal of Positive Behavior Interventions, 17*, 28–38. https://doi.org/10.1177/1098300713517141.

Minahan, J. (2019). Trauma-informed teaching strategies. *Educational Leadership, 77*, 30–35.

Nadeem, E., Mcnamee, E., Lang, J. M., Perry, D., & Lich, K. H. (2022). Novel application of system support mapping for sustainment of trauma-focused mental health intervention in school-based health centers: A case study. *Evidence-Based*

Practice in Child and Adolescent Mental Health, 1–17. https://doi.org/10.1080/23 794925.2022.2056928.

Nocentini, A., Zambuto, V., & Menesini, E. (2015). Anti-bullying programs and Information and Communication Technologies (ICTs): A systematic review. *Aggression and Violent Behavior, 23*, 52–60. https://doi.org/10.1016/j.avb.2015.05.012.

Noltemeyer, A., Palmer, K., James, A. G., & Wiechman, S. (2019). School-wide positive behavioral interventions and supports (SWPBIS): A synthesis of existing research. *International Journal of School & Educational Psychology, 7*, 253–62. https://doi.org/10.1080/21683603.2018.1425169.

O'Connor, C. A., Dyson, J., Cowdell, F., & Watson, R. (2018). Do universal school-based mental health promotion programmes improve the mental health and emotional wellbeing of young people? A literature review. *Journal of Clinical Nursing, 27*, e412–e426. https://doi.org/10.1111/jocn.14078.

O'Reilly, M., Svirydzenka, N., Adams, S., & Dogra, N. (2018). Review of mental health promotion interventions in schools. *Social Psychiatry and Psychiatric Epidemiology, 53*, 647–62. https://doi.org/10.1007/s00127-018-1530-1.

Papadopoulos, C., Lodder, A., Constantinou, G., & Randhawa, G. (2019). Systematic review of the relationship between autism stigma and informal caregiver mental health. *Journal of Autism and Developmental Disorders, 49*, 1665–85. https://doi.org/10.1007/s10803-018-3835-z.

Phelps, C., & Sperry, L. L. (2020). Children and the COVID-19 pandemic. *Psychological Trauma: Theory, Research, Practice, and Policy, 12*, S73–S75. https://doi.org/10.1037/tra0000861.

Reaves, S., Bohnenkamp, J., Mayworm, A., Sullivan, M., Connors, E., Lever, N., . . . & Hoover, S. (2022). Associations between school mental health team membership and impact on service provision. *School Mental Health*, 1–13. https://doi.org/10.1007/s12310-021-09493-z.

Rice, K. L., Miller, G. F., Coronado, F., & Meltzer, M. I. (2020). Estimated resource costs for implementation of CDC's recommended COVID-19 mitigation strategies in pre-kindergarten through grade 12 public schools—United States, 2020–21 school year. *Morbidity and Mortality Weekly Report, 69*, 1917. https://doi.org/10.15585/mmwr.mm6950e1.

Salloum, A., & Overstreet, S. (2012). Grief and trauma intervention for children after disaster: Exploring coping skills versus trauma narration. *Behaviour Research and Therapy, 50*, 169–79. https://doi.org/10.1016/j.brat.2012.01.001.

Sanchez, A. L., Cornacchio, D., Poznanski, B., Golik, A. M., Chou, T., & Comer, J. S. (2018). The effectiveness of school-based mental health services for elementary-aged children: A meta-analysis. *Journal of the American Academy of Child & Adolescent Psychiatry, 57*, 153–65. https://doi.org/10.1016/j.jaac.2017.11.022.

Santiago, C. D., Raviv, T., & Jaycox, L. H. (2018). *Creating healing school communities: School-based interventions for students exposed to trauma*. Washington, DC: American Psychological Association.

Sinclair, A. C., Gesel, S. A., & Lemons, C. J. (2019). The effects of peer-assisted learning on disruptive behavior and academic engagement. *Journal of Positive Behavior Interventions, 21*, 238–48. https://doi.org/10.1177/1098300719851227.

Soneson, E., Howarth, E., Ford, T., Humphrey, A., Jones, P. B., Thompson Coon, J., . . . & Anderson, J. K. (2020). Feasibility of school-based identification of children and adolescents experiencing, or at-risk of developing, mental health difficulties: A systematic review. *Prevention Science, 21*, 581–603. https://doi.org/10.1007/s11121-020-01095-6.

Stoiber, K. C., & Gettinger, M. (2016). Multi-tiered systems of support and evidence-based practices. In M. K. Jimerson, A. M. Burns, & A.M. VanDerHeyden (Eds.), *The handbook of response to intervention: The science and practice of multi-tiered systems of support*, second edition (pp. 121–41). New York: Springer.

Stratford, B., Cook, E., Hanneke, R., Katz, E., Seok, D., Steed, H., . . . & Temkin, D. (2020). A scoping review of school-based efforts to support students who have experienced trauma. *School Mental Health, 12*, 442–77. https://doi.org/10.1007/s12310-020-09368-9.

Sulkowski, M. L., Joyce, D. K., & Storch, E. A. (2012). Treating childhood anxiety in schools: Service delivery in a response to intervention paradigm. *Journal of Child and Family Studies, 21*, 938–47. https://doi.org/10.1007/s10826-011-9553-1.

Swick, D., & Powers, J. D. (2018). Increasing access to care by delivering mental health services in schools: The school-based support program. *School Community Journal, 28*, 129–44.

Tingey, L., Chambers, R., Patel, H., Littlepage, S., Lee, S., Lee, A., . . . & Rosenstock, S. (2021). Prevention of sexually transmitted diseases and pregnancy prevention among Native American youths: A randomized controlled trial, 2016–2018. *American Journal of Public Health, 111*, 1874–84. https://doi.org/10.2105/AJPH.2021.306447.

US Department of Education (2016). *The state of racial diversity in the educator workforce*. Washington, DC: Author.

Van Ryzin, M. J., Roseth, C. J., Fosco, G. M., Lee, Y. K., & Chen, I. C. (2016). A component-centered meta-analysis of family-based prevention programs for adolescent substance use. *Clinical Psychology Review, 45*, 72–80. https://doi.org/10.1016/j.cpr.2016.03.007.

Voith, L. A., Yoon, S., Topitzes, J., & Brondino, M. J. (2020). A feasibility study of a school-based social emotional learning program: Informing program development and evaluation. *Child and Adolescent Social Work Journal, 37*, 329–42. https://doi.org/10.1007/s10560-019-00634-7.

Walkington, C., & Bernacki, M. L. (2020). Appraising research on personalized learning: Definitions, theoretical alignment, advancements, and future directions. *Journal of Research on Technology in Education, 52*, 235–52. https://doi.org/10.1080/15391523.2020.1747757.

World Health Organization (2019). *School-based violence prevention: A practical handbook*. Switzerland: Author.

Yoder, C. M. (2020). School nurses and student academic outcomes: An integrative review. *Journal of School Nursing, 36*, 49–60. https://doi.org/10.1177/1059840518824397.

Chapter 5

Lessons Learned by Leading during COVID

Allison Arnold-Kempers, Matthew Wojas,
Alyssa Preddie Allen, Denver Wade,
and Sara Lauerman

In the late spring and early summer of 2020, schools in Indiana, and across the United States, were in a period of uncertainty. Indiana governor Eric Holcomb had ordered closure of all school buildings and in-person instruction after an initial pause to in-person learning in order to flatten the initial COVID-19 curve in mid-March.

For members of Butler University's Experiential Program for Preparing School Principals (EPPSP), this time had added questions for members as both leaders within their school buildings and as students themselves. The program originally had summer plans for members to visit Italy and research educational systems within the country; however, this prospect vanished as the specter of COVID-19 covered both countries. In this setting, Professor Debra Lecklider, head of EPPSP, crafted a summer course that could address every member's situation and serve as a resource to any K–12 school within Indiana or any of the other fifty states. The final product of this course was to be *The EPPSP Blueprint 2020: A Guidebook for School Leaders Moving Forward*. Within this guide, groups within the cohort would address the following areas: finance, athletics, equity, transportation, operations, parent/community/engagement, remediation/instruction, technology, curriculum, professional development, domestic and international considerations, social-emotional learning/trauma, and scheduling. While each group would be focusing on its own area of individual area of expertise, every member was guided in the methodology for the research—governed in the process of design thinking.

What follows immediately will be an overview in the methods of design thinking; proceeding afterward will be the research of members of the Equity Team along with their own personal experience implementing these within their public school settings from preschool level through high school. Finally, team members will leave suggestions for future adverse events that affect schools.

THE EPPSP BLUEPRINT 2020 EQUITY TEAM EXPERIENCE

Utilizing the design thinking process helped the Equity Team to find opportunity in the constantly shifting valley of the unknown, in which data was ever-changing, shifting, or nonexistent. The biggest opportunity lay in the team being able to identify and highlight structural inequities and improve these systems where inequities existed. A question that guided the group was whether or not there were inequities between a broken-down subgroup and the overall population in terms of student achievement.

From this process, the Equity Team synthesized findings and helped to create action plans to address systemic inequity within the following populations: special education students, emergent bilingual students, high-ability students, and financially underresourced students. While proud of the research, action plans, and publication, the team also continued in the design thinking process implementing these strategies and constantly adjusting and refining them within their schools as teachers, leaders, and administrators. What follows will be experiences, successes, and learnings from each member from the first half of the 2020–2021 school year.

Key Takeaways from the EPPSP Blueprint 2020

Educational equity is not an additional aspect to any of the other research in the *EPPSP 2020*. Instead, it encompasses and is interwoven with every single facet of education. As educators, our mission is to guarantee the facilitation of learning to all students, regardless of family background, race, culture, economic status, or sexual orientation. For many years, education has systematically not always lived up to this broad mission. Problems in ensuring learning for all students were exacerbated with the COVID-19 pandemic. Not all students had equitable access to technology; beyond just academics, minority and economically underresourced communities were more strongly affected by the virus. Students, and the United States of America as a whole, experienced trauma with the unrest based in racial tension as the summer started. With this understanding, schools can no longer idly sit by and hold different standards for students based on their backgrounds. Our work outlined how we as educators can use this opportunity to improve education and equitably address all students now and in the future.

Special Education

While all of education was thrown into the unknown with the spread of COVID-19, the world of special education was most affected. Special education addresses the needs of students with disabilities and provides support for these students to best learn while they gain skills and achieve goals based on their individual needs. These services are legally mandated across the country, federally coded in IDEA. Due to this legal nature, special education has traditionally been an area rife with litigation. The absence of in-person learning may exacerbate the contentiousness of this realm (one interviewed local school board attorney anticipated "an avalanche of lawsuits"). While it is important that school leaders are aware of this, they must also keep in mind their moral duty to best serve all students moving forward, finding collaborative, creative ways to do so with special education teachers, content area teachers, and families. As this will remain a "gray area" as we move forward into the 2020–21 academic year, we must remember to have a "north star" of guiding principles and do everything within our means to give our special education students what they need. Key ideas from our research are noted here.

What Has Happened

- Special education is a federally mandated program; however, there has been minimum federal guidance during the COVID-19 pandemic. This has put more stress on state departments of education and local school districts in coming up with ways to best serve their students.
- In many schools throughout the state and the country, services were at the minimum altered; in certain situations, some services could not be fulfilled due to unforeseen limitations.
- Evaluations could not be conducted appropriately, creating a backlog for the new school year.

What to Expect and How Leaders Can Address This

- Special education teachers will be the busiest people in the school upon return. Administration must support them as they work through this process.
- While learning gaps may have developed among many students, we must not disservice the students or the adults by overdiagnosing learning disabilities. Those students with disabilities absolutely must be serviced, and every student must have his/her needs met, but that does not necessarily have to be with an IEP.
- School leaders should leverage the CARES Act for funding, including the utilization of the school nurse into plans.

- Development of instructional aides and provision for reliable services and training (especially for an e-learning context) for them is important to fulfilling our duty to special education students.

EMERGENT BILINGUAL

As schools shut down in the spring, many emergent bilingual students left the only place in which they were formally instructed in English. While school leaders may be concerned about a possible lack of growth in these students' English skills, they must not create the narratives for these students, who may still have been learning English with their families and/or translating for their families. Also, these students were able to develop skills in their native language if they were with family members who did not speak English. Upon return to school, this idea of developing bilingual students in a holistic fashion must be emphasized, and the concept of monolingual instruction only valuing English should be eliminated, not only for the immediate effects of valuing these students but also for the long-term effects of their development.

What Has Happened

- Prior to COVID-19, the world of English learners (ELs), or emergent bilingual students, has been the least understood in a general education setting due to a lack of training in traditional educator prep programs.
- Many content area teachers within a school do not understand the importance of the emergent bilingual teacher. Traditional educational leadership programs have neglected this as well.
- While emergent bilingual instruction is now being paid more attention by state departments of education, there is not a national framework as with special education. Many states and corporations have a lack of uniformity in addressing emergent bilingual students.
- As there is not a uniform model, some schools still have used a pullout model, which is neither just for the bilingual students nor for the nonbilingual students in the classroom.

What to Expect and How Leaders Can Address This

- Leadership from the emergent bilingual teacher will be paramount for these students' growth. Teacher leadership in this area utilizes "creativity,

resistance, and advocacy" (Morita-Mullaney, 2019, p. 1). Administration can help foster this leadership by regularly meeting with the emergent bilingual teachers and setting up times for the emergent bilingual teachers to work with content area teachers. Additional supports to assist with the emergent bilingual teachers' time must be provided (Champion).
- Using only a pullout model for emergent bilingual students could hinder development upon return to school. Inclusion creates more belonging and helps to develop true bilingualism (Morita-Mullaney, 2019).
- School administration must foster a culture in which emergent bilingual teachers are viewed as a coteacher or outright teacher, not as aides or instructional assistants.
- School administration must allow for greater advocacy from teachers of emergent bilingual students in order to best facilitate these students and empower their learning.

FINANCIALLY MARGINALIZED STUDENTS

"We are all in the same storm, but on different ships." This metaphor paints a picture of how all students experienced trauma in some form or other with the cancellation of in-person schooling; however, some students went home to stable, food-secure, connected environments able to facilitate continued learning. On the other hand, many students faced increased food insecurity and/or a lack of internet connectivity, creating inequitable situations for their learning. Many students in a high-poverty environment also face unhealthy living conditions, causing detriment to their learning, both in school and now at home. Student connectivity and health will have to be major focus points for school leaders as we move forward.

What Has Happened

- E-learning was as good as it could have been under the circumstances in which the need arose; however, connectivity problems created a gap for students who could not access resources.
- Unhealthy living conditions have always played a role in student achievement (eight trips to the school nurse is equivalent with eight points lower achievement on standardized testing (Rattermann et al., 2020); some students have been living in these conditions, now no longer even leaving them for school.

What to Expect and How Leaders Can Address This

- Student Connectivity
    - Finding a solution for connectivity is vital. Two possible ways (of many) to do this follow: first, a school can invest in mobile hotspots that are based on a cell phone payment plan; second, a secured school-only network for all student homes can be created so that students could have access to the same web resources that they have at school.
    - Schools and teacher training programs must address e-learning best practices with teachers; schools must facilitate online communities of practice.
- Student Health
    - Schools should use available health data in MTSS/RTI process.
    - A school nurse is a valuable asset. Every school should make having a school nurse a top priority. A school may pay for a nurse using moneys from the general fund or by partnering with a local hospital who supplies the necessary services.
    - A school nurse's data is important; therefore, the nurse must be involved in a school's academic plan/SIP.

TEACHING DURING COVID: A TEACHER'S PERSPECTIVE

The experience of being an educator, student, parent, and maintaining a social life during the pandemic was an experience that forever changed us all. Managing the family and work-life balance was a struggle as we became adapted to video conferencing and working from home. In the area of early childhood education, the need for hands-on in-person learning is apparent; however, we were able to be creative in our instruction and support to families by utilizing local and national grant resources along with districtwide meal delivery programs. Being unable to fulfill my need for social interaction and being around other human beings during the pandemic left me feeling melancholy and stale. By utilizing technology and local partnerships I found that volunteering, porch drop off of supplies, and meeting the needs of the students virtually or from their porch helped fill the void left due to the pandemic.

As educators and leaders we have learned that flexibility and remembering your *mission and vision* are tools that can lift you up when you are down. By demonstrating positive leadership and modeling your *mission and vision*, you can lift up your team and focus on what the community needs during desperate times. Kindness and grace are important steps at fostering relationships with stakeholders.

Technology in an Early Childhood Setting

The impacts of COVID-19 on students in early childhood education in special education and ELL programs became evident as it placed a spotlight on the many inequities and inconsistencies that are present in meeting the unique needs of special needs and ELL students in a remote and hybrid learning environment. COVID-19 helped bring awareness to issues of inequity of student access to technology and the internet, as well as other socioeconomic challenges that impact student learning and success in school. Federal policies such as NCLB and ESSA (Every Student Succeeds Act [December 2015]) have been developed to address the issue of providing appropriate education for students, while also ensuring that the appropriate supports are provided for students receiving special education and ELL services in an in-person learning environment. It became evident that there were unaddressed needs for early childhood in ELL students, special needs, and students from diverse socioeconomic backgrounds who were facing enormous challenges that NCLB and ESSA did not begin to address. As educators began remote and hybrid instruction, the challenge of providing special services remotely for early childhood students with special needs and early childhood ELLs proved to be far more significant than any current regulations have ever addressed. Equitable access is the guarantee that all students are provided the necessary and individualized supplementary aids and services, accommodations, modifications, or supports to meaningfully participate in the general education curriculum.

COVID-19 restrictions made service provision and student skill assessment a challenge that many educators had never faced. Students did not have access to equipment, learning tools, assistive devices, as well as specialized and trained personnel, from whom they received daily physical support. Local leaders quickly set up policies and procedures to remotely address and meet the needs of students with special needs and ELL in an attempt to ensure standards and individual education plan goals would continue to be met. This brought on additional challenges as many staff were attempting to familiarize themselves with new technology and support families as they navigated the same new technology. Students went without equipment, learning tools, and physical support from personnel due to COVID restrictions, and, in some cases, there were limited resources available to school systems. Local agencies did not provide additional financial resources to school districts to provide the resources that this special population of students needed for continued skill development and academic success. The heightened awareness of inequities has resulted in an increase in resources and professional development opportunities that will help teachers utilize strategies that will improve the support necessary to help ELL students develop their L2 skills for improved success in classrooms that are predominantly presented in the L1. Additionally, many school systems have applied for grant funding that allows them to obtain resources to support students with special needs in a remote and hybrid learning environment. Service providers in the school system formulated plans to provide resources such as computers, tablets and access to internet services for students with special needs. These efforts are a good start to reducing and eventually eliminating the inequities that COVID-19 has highlighted.

COVID-19 has also illuminated the gaps among the diverse populations in our classrooms across America. For many early childhood ELL students, the dominant language in the classroom and remote learning environment is English and the support necessary for their academic success was not available in the remote and hybrid learning environment. This additional communication issue has a greater impact as these students navigate remote and hybrid learning environments. Many families are unable to provide support to their children as they are not fluent in English either. Providing support for all ELL students was not equitable in many remote and hybrid learning environments. In some cases limited access to trained support staff is the issue and, in others, the financial resources to provide this support was not available or services are not yet available at all.

All students deserve an education that addresses their individual needs. COVID-19 opens up the issue of providing appropriate support in a virtual environment equal to that which is mandated for the classrooms our special needs and ELL students participate in. Giving content through interactive engaging virtual and visual content is one strategy that will provide support in a virtual classroom for ELL students. While not ideal, programs like Kahoot, Flipgrid, Google Classroom, Moodle, Zoom, and Jamboard are just a few tools that can be utilized to assist students in video read alouds and choral reading and provide authentic conversations that allow early childhood special education and ELL students to continue to make progress their individual goals.

As we reflect on the impact COVID-19 has had on many students and school systems throughout the state of Indiana, we recognize the need to include all stakeholders. Teachers, students, parents, school leaders, local leadership, and community partners all play a role in ensuring the diverse needs for students' schools are met. We recognize that teachers, students, and parents may need to utilize many different portions of the curriculum with individualized options offered to meet the specific needs of all.

Virtual Learning in a Small School Setting

When COVID hit, I was in my sixth year of teaching at a trauma-informed school district on the southeast side of a large urban city. I teach fifth-grade math in an intermediate building serving grades 4, 5, and 6. My district serves around 60 percent of students that are considered to be economically disadvantaged. All my six years of teaching have been in an inclusive classroom. When March 2020 happened, my mind went in a million different directions. I not only was working with an extremely vulnerable and diverse population but also the added factors of meeting the needs of my special education students. We did not have a plan, nor were we receiving any type of guidance on how to handle this new norm with such a vulnerable population. The spring of 2020 was complete survival mode. What follows are my learnings and personal takeaways from summer research with *The EPPSP Blueprint*; afterwards I will relate how I was able to use these learnings in our new setting of the 2020–2021 school year.

In March 2020, educators all around the world were thrust into the unknown after navigating the uncharted territory of the COVID-19 pandemic. We went from hectic days of planning the upcoming state standardized testing schedule and navigating small groups in the classroom to transitioning to solely digital learning models that we had no previous experience in. As a group of driven educators currently working on our master's degrees, we became enthralled with the facts being vocalized to us and what the future state would hold for educators everywhere. We heard from state leaders, superintendents, college professors, and teachers that were in the trenches daily. We discussed everyone that was affected by this new norm and how the future would look for classroom teachers, school leaders, students, and families.

All areas of education were floundering in disadvantaged school corporations, whether it was the sudden halt of athletics, English language learners serviced by a platform not catered to their needs, or special education students whose needs were not being met due to the lack of guidance by the federal government. The reality in late spring is that this population of students would fall substantially behind that of their peers and that teachers were generating a backlog that they would be faced with in the upcoming school year.

Educators all over were struggling and fearing the future as they found ways to service their special education population. All over the country, services were being altered, and in some situations, services were left being unfulfilled due to the unforeseen circumstances. A population that is most vulnerable to educational disruptions and is federally mandated to receive service was getting absolutely zero guidance. Stressed state departments and local school districts were forced to act quickly on how to best service the most needed population. "One analysis of distance learning plans for all 50 states and the District of Columbia, the Center on Reinventing Public Education at the University of Washington . . . found that only 18 states, including Kentucky, require all districts to include special education in those plans" (Mitchell, 2020). How could we possibly open up schools in the fall when only eighteen states in the country seemed to care about the needs of our special education students?

Out of all the research that my team conducted through our reopening plan for schools, the most important pieces are those relating to the parent/teacher relationship and making sure that parents are involved in the process of making their child successful. Parental guidance had to be an utmost priority to protect not only the school district but also the students involved. Recommendations consist of weekly video updates from that child's team and making sure that parents are educated on jargon that may be used when referencing their child and how they can use their vocabulary to engage in conversation about their child.

It also becomes valuable that teachers are in strict communication with parents about the ever-changing improvements to the distance learning model. We knew going into this unusual situation that it was not going to be perfect, but we also knew it could only get better. If teachers plan to roll out a new learning model or online platform, they must be expected not only to teach the students these new tools, but they must also teach the parents, so they can assist their child at home. Teachers need to be upfront with parents about changes and limit them being in the dark so that it's not a shock when they sit down after a long day of work to help with homework.

Teachers and school psychologists should provide guidance on home routines, organization, and structure that will help develop a healthier and less chaotic or anxiety-filled learning reality. When teachers are in the classrooms, one will regularly see norms and schedules posted around the classroom to help keep students in order and remind them of expectations. Similar strategies can be used at the home level to help remind students that in their new norm, the only thing changing is the location.

On top of creating an environment conducive to learning, providing regular communication, and educating parents, it also becomes valuable to educate parents on how to deal with their students' fears and anxieties that stem from this new norm. One day students could be playing Pokémon on the playground with their friends and eating chicken nuggets in the cafeteria; suddenly, they could immediately be rushed into the reality of learning Google Classroom and Zoom and how to have exponentially more responsibility than they held the day before. Teachers need to help parents understand the basic foundational requirements in the development of self-esteem and building the actions to help their children through COVID-19 so they can better manage their anxieties, frustrations, and concerns. Whether we knew it or not, we all became a stronger team in March 2020. I look back on that regularly and ask myself what I would have done differently in the spring of 2020, not even just for my special education students but for all students. Providing parents with resources and support to make sure their child and they themselves are taken care of mentally, physically, and emotionally would have been my number one priority.

After the initial shock of the last eight weeks of the spring semester, we reset and prepared to enter the unknowns of what the new school year would look like. We began the 2020–2021 school year virtually under the orders of the mayor of Indianapolis. This would only last a week, though, and we used that week to prepare students and staff for the transition back into the school building the week of August 10.

Students and families were given the option to choose in-person or online learning for the first nine weeks. The expectation was that this choice would remain in effect for an entire grading period with zero change to that child's learning choice. With each of the grade levels split into teams of three, one teacher per team was assigned a "virtual" homeroom while the other teachers had in-person students. Because we rotated through teams for each subject, teachers would teach one class virtually and the remainder in person. Much of the planning that went into the new school year focused on in-person learning and not much consideration was paid to an entire virtual approach.

Looking back, this seemed like the most logical way to handle the 30 percent of students who were opting for the exclusively virtual option. My one virtual class a day allowed my attention to be focused on those students virtually without also having to double-dip with students in person. Going into the school year, we had two (out of three) teams in the fifth grade who had a caseload of special education students in the general classroom. When we realized the significant number of special education students who chose online learning to begin the school year, we shifted them all to one team: my team. One special education teacher was assigned all virtual students on her caseload between the three grade levels, while the other three teachers were assigned to the in-person students per each grade level. The in-person special education team worked as it had done in the past years—pushing in for small groups, pulling out students for extra time, running additional remediation groups, etc. The online special education teacher's duties were more challenging. It was a constant battle of tracking down students not attending class regularly, supporting students who needed that extra help 110 percent of the time, and keeping students in an online class for the entire time. One student in particular would not log into class without assistance from his parents, which created distractions in the classroom regularly. I would send one student daily to the breakout room on Google Meet for a small group and he would log off every time, never receiving his serviced minutes. The only way I know how to describe it was *a mess*.

As the first nine weeks dragged on what felt like an entire year, we also were facing the constant back and forth of what happens when students are quarantined or are considered a first close contact and sent home for two weeks. The wide list of COVID-19 symptoms also sent home kids daily. Due to HIPAA, we were not told why students were not coming to school or why they were sent home, just that they would be gone for an extended period. Those students were trained to jump into online school when those situations occurred, and they would stay within the same team of teachers they had when they were in person. This of course was easier said than done and by the time we helped parents get connected to Wi-Fi for those two weeks, quarantine for that student expired and they were back in school. I felt now that my most important job in the world was just keeping track of where my students were at all times, and that seemed endless. We were not prepared for the constant maneuvering of kids, while also doing our number one job: teaching.

When the city decided to push all schools virtual before Thanksgiving break until January 15, this once again flipped the tables. We had one week to prepare all students for going virtual. We split our caseload of special education students among two teams, assigning an instructional assistant per pod, as well as the teacher of record. Each of those teachers was given an iPad to help them conduct high-quality instruction. When the schedule was created for what virtual learning would look like, I made sure that appropriate time was given for students in breakout rooms to help accommodate their IEPs.

The virtual time spent before Christmas break only ignited my desire for students to return to the building safely. There was a high correlation among our students not attending regularly scheduled classes and those that had an IEP. Oftentimes I would send them to a breakout room, only for them to log off immediately. Students would log on and never respond, only to try and prove to their parents they were in class. Special blocks that were set up for remediation were never active because students were not joining for additional support. Parent response was mediocre, some very frustrated with both teachers and students, some frustrated with themselves, and some just flat out overwhelmed with navigating a pandemic with a child who requires extra attention. My parent contact log during the four weeks we were virtual before break was about five times as long as my contact list from the month of October alone.

I don't advocate for virtual learning as an option for all students. There are a lot of moving parts that constantly have to be intertwined such as parents, teachers, and the students' willingness to give effort on the other end. My students who have an IEP are the majority who already have inconsistent attendance and a home life with minimal resources available to them. Many of these same students have working parents with irregular hours that just could not prioritize their students' learning in the traditional sense. I had one student who was frequently not showing up and was being inappropriate when he did. We documented this behavior, as we did attendance (tracked the normal way through Skyward), and built a case to have this student brought into school to be monitored because virtual learning was not successful. Because this was a special case, transportation was not provided, but parents had no way of bringing him each day, so it fell through the wayside. This example, among many, is where I understood that virtual learning was not beneficial without the workings of all three parties involved.

A High School Perspective

The COVID-19 pandemic forced schools across the country and across the state of Indiana to reimagine instruction in less than ideal circumstances. While these times have made "normal" impossible to obtain for most schools, they have also made school leaders rethink what "normal" can be. In a certain sense, the pandemic conditions for learning have made education take a small step back, but this small step backward is a springboard for a great leap forward.

At our high school, our summer leadership meetings were based around two aspects—equity and our instructional model for the school year. Equity was key in everyone's mind. While the high school is considered a top school in Indiana for many reasons, including its AP program access and success, there are students who are not reaping the benefit of these educational outcomes. Specifically, students serviced in special education and students who come from a Latin American background, whether or not they are currently serviced as ELs. Figures 5.1 and 5.2 indicate the disparity in achievement on

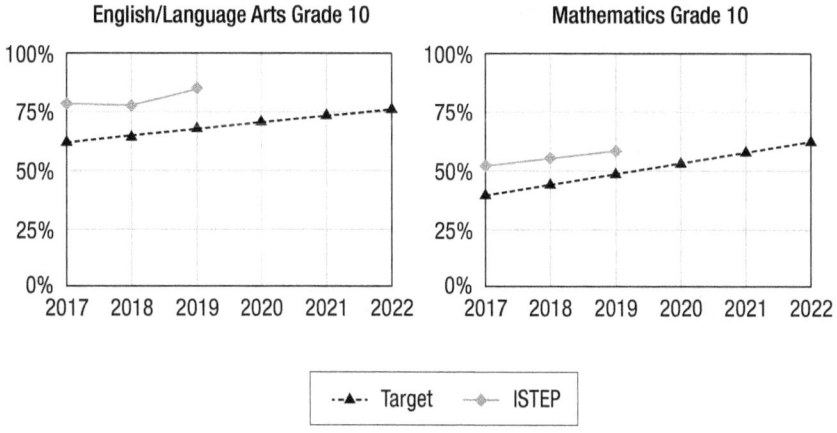

Figure 5.1. Student Performance

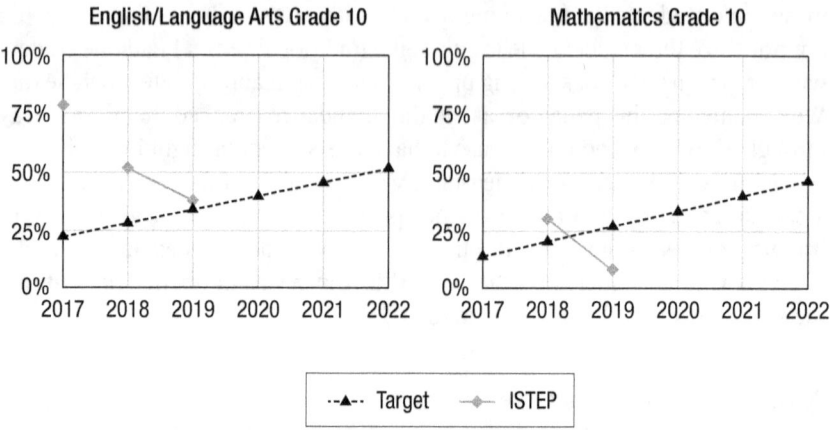

Figure 5.2. Special Education Pass Rates on Standardized Testing

standardized testing through Indiana's ISTEP +. Not only is there a gap in achievement, but the two-year trend demonstrates special education students' achievement going in a direction different than that of the entire school population as a whole.

Beyond this, students from Latin American backgrounds were disproportionately represented in discipline (specifically suspensions), attendance, lower test scores, and remedial course enrollment. Although the high school is a majority White school, Latin American students make up nearly 10 percent of the school's population. Eleven percent of the school at one point in their schooling has been labeled an EL and has had an ILP. Our free and reduced lunch students also fell well below overall school results as indicated by the achievement scores shown in figure 5.3.

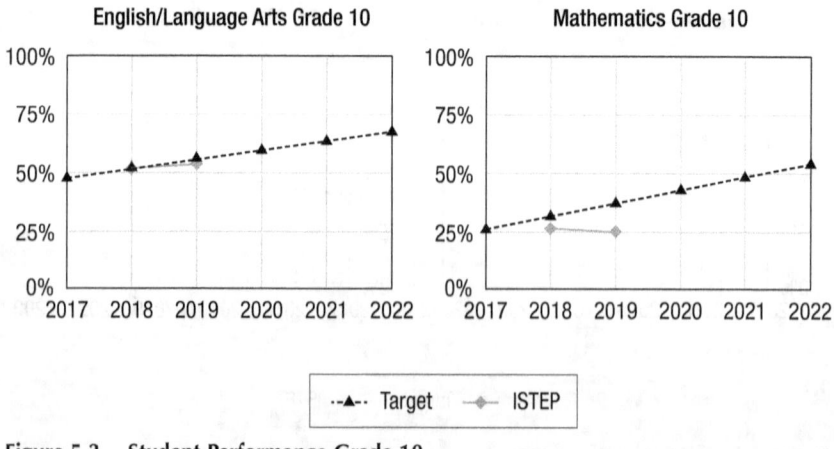

Figure 5.3. Student Performance Grade 10

Nearby districts had recently established their schedules, choosing a hybrid schedule. As a high school team, we were to meet and discuss options, focusing mostly on the best possible hybrid schedule for all students within our building. Each building leadership team would then bring their best plans to a districtwide meeting before the district created its final plans. The meeting was structured by first allowing each member to pick a lens with which to view schedule possibilities. Lenses chosen included the following:

- Cynical
- Marginalized students
- Equity
- Teacher workload (multiple preps)
- Students who do not thrive in e-learning format
- Athletics
- Extracurricular activities
- Reasonable (science)—not letting fears control us
- Exceptional learners
- Wellness leaf

My lens was that of looking at how the new hybrid schedule could affect traditionally marginalized students. Before diving into our options, we then reestablished what our school's mission and vision were and what were key elements of school culture. These key culture elements were meant to center our work.

Our Schools Vision/Mission:

- Move heaven and earth
- No one is expendable
- Prepare kids for day after graduation
- All means all
- Emphasis on rigor
- Collaborative culture
- Relationships based
- Life ready

After these establishments, the *why* behind a hybrid schedule was established. Concerns for social distancing within the building, especially for situations with COVID-19 spikes, were at the forefront for the hybrid model. Meeting participants then delved into survey data taken from both staff and parents. These data points allowed us to understand concerns that participants had moving into the new school year full of unknowns.

The bulk of the meeting then examined the pros and cons of each hybrid schedule suggested. The four options follow:

Option A: Students alternate attendance daily, five days per week. One cohort will attend school in person three times in one week and then twice the next, with the other cohort having the same schedule. Virtual learning will take place on days in which cohort members are not in the building.

Option B: Students alternate attendance by cohort weekly. One cohort will be in the school building five times one week and will do all virtual learning the next week.

Option C: Students will alternate daily over the course of four days, with a fifth day as an exclusive virtual learning day.

Option D: Students will alternate after two days of in-person schooling. Cohort A will attend school on two consecutive days; Cohort B will attend school on two consecutive days. One day per week will be exclusive for virtual learning.

In looking at all these options, the two that all committee members thought strongest were Option A and Option C. Option A was desirable for the extra time in which students and teachers would be face to face. Option C was desirable for built-in time for teachers to develop quality instruction on both in-person and virtual platforms. With much discussion, the committee ultimately decided upon Option C, *if* and only *if* students could come into the building on the afternoon of the all virtual day for remediation and enrichment with teachers or for school club opportunities with transportation provided. "Make it meaningful!" was the rallying cry upon the end of the meeting. The district meeting with secondary schools (intermediate school: a grades 5 and 6 building; middle school: a grades 7 and 8 building) established a unanimous support for this schedule, and the buildings created a final schedule that has been employed throughout the entirety of the school year to date (through winter break).

With this new schedule, we as school leaders had to be very deliberate in living out our vision of equity and being sure that this would work for all students. It was decided in this meeting that all EL students at a 1 or 2 in world-class instructional design and assessment (WIDA) composites would be welcomed and encouraged to come into the building four days per week in order to have more built-in support face to face with content area teachers and more supports with their language lab. Language acquisition was in mind with this decision (being in-person allows for more conversation and word acquisition as gestures and vocal tone are a large part of learning a language) as was providing the best opportunity for these students to have access to teachers, resources, and any other supports. The school had just hired two instructional aides fluent in Spanish and Egyptian Arabic, our two most represented languages among our ELs. These instructional aides would be able to assist in language lab as well as go to content area classes to assist our EL students.

In order to broadcast this out fully, the school organized a parental outreach night at a local park across the street from the high school. Helping to facilitate was a native Spanish speaker and a known and respected member of the town's Latin American community. The outreach was held at a park in order to help families feel safe and secure not entering into close quarters within a building during the pandemic. Though the park was near the high school, it was also near a large community of Latin American students—well within walking distance.

Upon the trimester break (mid-November), data helped to support that the four-day-per-week program instituted for WIDA 1s and 2s had been successful. EL supports for students at WIDA levels 3 through 5 had also been effective; in an analysis of students with multiple Fs, a very small fraction was represented by our students who had been enrolled as a student within the EL program.

Special education also had similar strategies to address this schedule. While all Free Assistance Program (FAP) and life skills students (nondiploma track students) were enrolled four days per week in self-contained classrooms, inclusion students were on the alternating days hybrid. Westfield High School uses a basic skills development (BSD) model (resource period) in order to implement special education services. Very quickly, some BSD teachers saw the negative effects of the hybrid on their students' learning. Just like our students in EL with WIDA 1s and 2s, special education students were invited to come into the school building four days per week in order to provide a better environment for learning with more controls and supports in place. This did not change a special education student's LRE as only the location of the supports changed. The student would be in BSD whether or not in person, so the amount of time enrolled in the course did not change. The biggest difference was seeing teachers, both content area and BSD, on a consistent daily basis. At trimester, students on this plan had demonstrated much more success than they initially had on the alternating hybrid.

As a result, we opened this option up to other special education students and to students who did not demonstrate success on the hybrid schedule. I was to create and oversee this system for our students who would be in the building every day of in-person learning. I collaborated with school counselors and teachers to identify the students who would best benefit from this. I also examined the list of students with multiple Fs. In identifying these students, it was important to also build a relationship with them. As part of the system, I would meet with all students who were entering into the building four days per week (unless, as noted, they were being overseen by EL or special education). One of the governing philosophies on student-teacher relationships at the high school is that every young person needs a Power of 5—a network of five caring, trusted adults within that young person's life. While we hope that all students have a number of the Power of 5 outside of the school, we cannot assume anything and therefore work to ensure that students would name teachers and staff at the high school as a major part of their Power of 5. With this as my guide, I wanted to be sure that all these students who had not thrived in the hybrid environment would consider me as a part of their Power of 5. We met and held a goal-planning session individually. I also developed a system for more point people in counseling or administration to meet with these students and employ interventions as needed, all grounded in building a Power of 5.

For each check-in, the administrator or counselor holding the meeting will complete the form shown in textbox 5.1. As part of this, we will be analyzing which interventions work best. This is part of a larger, non-COVID-related plan that will serve all our students for years to come—the continued creation, refinement, and broadcast of a schoolwide multitiered system of supports. In the 2019–2020 school year, a basic plan was created; however, it has not spread throughout the entire school. With these students, we will be evaluating which interventions are most effective and from which tier most interventions come.

TEXTBOX 5.1.
Student Progress Monitoring Sheet

Student Name: _____

Student's Goals for Tri 2

Conference Date: _____

Notes (know grades before meeting with student; check to see how student is doing personally, in extracurriculars, and in classes):

_____

_____

Interventions employed (highlight):

- ☐ Organizational strategies
- ☐ Assigned targeted CORE (please schedule with no override option)
- ☐ Plug into tutoring
- ☐ Parental call
    - ☐ Positive praise
    - ☐ New plan outline
- ☐ Assigned Friday time
- ☐ Reward for progress
- ☐ Reteaching
- ☐ Counselor check-in

Follow-through items for next meeting (please limit to three):

_____

_____

_____

While the implementation of current systems and future systems for all our students brings excitement, as a school leader, I must be cognizant also of the here and now. While bringing students in for more support should yield better results, we must remember the entire purpose of the hybrid environment is to have class safely with effective social distancing to lower the spread of COVID-19. It is important that students and teachers both feel safe in order to learn and facilitate learning. As this is the case, students added to the four-day-per-week plan are being picked judiciously further, with clear criteria for being a part of the program, parental and teacher support. Looking at every single class and its numbers is vital to not overload any single class; scheduling is crucial for this plan to work. Another aspect to remember is that the hybrid schedule has changed how teachers teach. With two platforms for learning (in-person and virtual), teachers have gone above and beyond to make education meaningful on each. Some teachers mirror their virtual lessons (asynchronous) with their in-class sessions; others use a flipped model with a repeated lesson for in-person learners and an asynchronous different lesson for the virtual students on each day. With this in mind, it is important that teachers maximize the experience of students who are in the building four days per week. The memo shown in textbox 5.2 was sent out toward the beginning of trimester 2 in order to help teachers as they worked through yet another (important) addition to their plates for 2020.

TEXTBOX 5.2.

First, read *this spreadsheet* to identify which of your students are coming to school four days per week. **PowerSchool is currently updating.** When update is complete, these students will be labeled like this: **Day: Gold/Green**

Then ask yourself, "What style of class do I have with the hybrid schedule?"

1. If green and gold days have a new lesson every day, then you may continue that model, working deliberately with the students who are now four-day-per-week students.
2. If green and gold days repeat lessons (flipped classroom aspect), then there are various strategies to use within the class.

    A. Create an environment in which you are delivering the in-person lesson on both days, but your four-day-per-week student is accessing the online content on day 2. Be sure to check in with your student on their understanding and continue to build a relationship, as many students are here for both extra support and motivation.
    B. Sometimes the student may receive the same lesson, but you may differentiate with remediation or enrichment as needed based on the students' understanding of a concept.
    C. Does the student need extra time to master a skill? You can coordinate with BSD, Academy, or EL in order for that student to work with the support teachers. If a possibility, certain days the student may go with their support teacher for that period in order to complete work, take a test, work on a project, etc.

Right now, it is imperative to create a welcoming environment for *all* our students. What can you do to be a part of a student's Power of 5?

- Build relationships. Learn about the student, their likes and dislikes, especially regarding academics.
- What motivators can you tap into? Every student has something that helps motivate achievement. As you get to know your students, find those motivators.
- Reach out to students' TOR or overseeing administrator to collaborate, bounce questions, and/or problem solve. We are in this together!
- As attendance on PowerSchool gets sorted out, please do not single out students who are present on a day that is not their traditional team. If you have questions, please refer back to the spreadsheet.

The year 2020 was not an easy year for anybody. As a school, we are blessed to be safely in session; we are blessed as educators to see our students in person, and we are blessed to have our current challenges. With these challenges, we will grow and improve the experience for all our learners in our mission.

An Urban Teacher's Perspective

At the outset of the pandemic in Indiana, there were absolutely no data points upon which to base decisions. In March 2020, when the pandemic first directly impacted the district, we had the "luxury" of a two-week spring break to determine our plan for what we thought was only going to be two weeks out of the building in order to flatten the curve of the virus spreading. Those weeks stretched into May, which quickly morphed into the entire fourth quarter of our school year. Throughout this period of time we had only a handful of teachers designing/creating recorded lessons and assignments for each subject while other teachers in the district served as liaisons of those lessons. Teachers were only required to be on Zoom from 9:00 a.m. to 10:00 a.m. on Monday, Wednesday, and Friday for our SEL Core Connect classes. On Tuesdays and Thursdays, teachers were required to be logged into Zoom from 9:00 a.m. to 12:00 p.m. for "office hours" to answer questions regarding the video lessons/assignments, to which we did not have access prior to the actual posting of the lessons (which occurred every Monday morning). Students also weren't being held accountable for any of the work they completed and weren't receiving a grade for what they turned in. We knew that this educational model was ineffective and unsuccessful for students, especially because this model led to the decline of student attendance and learning.

As the summer wore on into the beginning of the school year, not much was known from the teacher perspective about what the upcoming school year was going to look like. The media was not the best source of information or data so we were mainly relying on state and local data and information in regard to COVID and school. We found out a few weeks before the beginning of the school year that we were returning to school under a hybridized schedule with a virtual option. Instead of returning on our normal start date of July 30, the start date was pushed back one week to August 6 to give time for teachers to recalibrate their planning and administrators and counselors to develop a new master schedule.

The Plan

The district plan was titled S.A.F.E. Reopening, with S.A.F.E. representing the following:

- Safety of students/staff
- Academics, athletics, and extracurriculars
- Facilities and operations
- Equitable access and outcomes

All planning was done with "fluidity" in mind in the situation that there would need to be change at a moment's notice. Certainly, there were constant changes as the plan was implemented. Just as in the design thinking process, there were many opportunities for trial and error. The initial plan utilized two cohorts in a hybrid model. In order for students to have equitable access to virtual learning from home, the district issued a Chromebook and an internet hotspot to students. The students were divided into their cohorts by last name; one cohort would report into the building three times per week on one week, then twice the next, with the other cohort reversing the order. With this five-day-per-week model, time was to be allotted with two to three days for instruction (could be either in-person or virtual) and two to three days for application.

Teachers were utilized in myriad ways. Some teachers were responsible for all virtual content, and the rest had one to two virtual periods while being responsible for a remainder of in-person learning. For direct instruction, teachers were to use both in-person opportunities and Zoom (called virtual in-person); math and ELA teachers who teach eighty-minute blocks also used this time for reteaching and remediation along with providing students with their application day practice assignment. Application days were days on which students would not report to school in person nor attend any Zoom session. Students would be applying knowledge to assignments posted on Canvas, a virtual learning platform.

With so many new variants introduced by the schedule, one point of major concern became attendance and engagement. No model has yet proven to be very effective. Originally, students had to complete an exit ticket created by the teacher on Canvas. There was much inconsistency with this model; therefore, this was scrapped in favor of a new plan with students taking their own attendance on their application days. Students would log into Canvas and take their attendance; however, this did not ensure actual engagement. While Canvas does provide data on student time logged in, this can be manipulated by opening the Canvas page on one tab of a laptop and keeping it open while actually engaging with anything else on or off the computer.

The overall teacher process for taking attendance proved to be a major headache as well. For the first month of the school year, every student was counted as present due to Zoom issues. After these issues had been resolved, teachers then took attendance for both virtual and in-person attendees. This proved to be a convoluted process. Teachers had to divide attendance into in-person and virtual cohorts and mark only the in-person cohort as present or absent. Application day students would be counted as all present and would be then changed to absent if the students did not complete the aforementioned exit ticket posted to Canvas. This was the system for hybrid students; however, there were also students who had elected to only take part in schooling through an all virtual option. Attendance for these students was a very complex problem. All students on the exclusively virtual plan would be counted automatically as PV—present virtual. Zoom students were counted as present provided they had logged onto Zoom. There was no other criteria. Students did not have to engage on Zoom, nor did they have to log onto Canvas. Their attendance was based solely on being logged into the Zoom session at any point in the lesson, even if it was for a negligible amount of time. For all virtual students, attendance for application days was still based on the completion of the aforementioned exit ticket.

The hybrid system and attendance odyssey that accompanied it continued after fall break. The new adjustment was that one cohort would attend school in person Monday, Wednesday, and every other Friday; its counterpart would attend school in person on Tuesday, Thursday, and the alternating Fridays. Students were responsible for taking their own attendance as this new system rolled out. In November, the County Health Department mandated that all schools in Indianapolis no longer hold school in person. Once again, schools would have to shift to an exclusively virtual platform after November 30. Attendance became based only on whether students had logged onto a teacher's Zoom; while reliable from a teacher perspective, this did not help to create engagement, as students still could be logged in for a negligible amount of time in order to be counted as present.

As the semester ended, yet another plan was put into place for the second half of the school year. Under this plan, both cohorts of students would combine for virtual days and attend Zoom classes on Mondays, Wednesdays, and Fridays. On Tuesdays and Thursdays, Learning Hubs would be facilitated. Learning Hubs were meant to provide supports and interventions, especially for students served in special education and EL.

Student Supports and Interventions within the Hybrid

Within our school's hybrid approach, supports for students were built in the following ways. For seventh-grade special education students, there was one main resource teacher paired with one instructional assistant. Just like all other students, the students served with special education were on the every-other-day hybrid schedule. The resource teacher was present in two blocks of ELA and two blocks of math, which are designed as direct coteaching classes. The instructional assistant supported the resource elective classes, science, social studies, as well as virtual resource class for application day students. There was no coteaching for science or social studies.

SUGGESTIONS FOR SCHOOLS IN FUTURE SITUATIONS WITH MASS EFFECTS

> Plans are nothing. Planning is everything.
>
> —Dwight Eisenhower

It is impossible and inefficient to dedicate time and energy to anticipate the next global catastrophe and have a specific plan for a school in such a circumstance; however, not preparing and using current data to address the constantly shifting needs of a school and its growth is a travesty in and of itself. A school must always be prepared by constantly engaging in design thinking with the goal of bettering itself for its clients—the students, their parents, and the community as a whole. It is important that schools always remember their *why*—often expressed in their mission and vision. These should not merely be words that are barely read on the school's website; instead, they should be foremost in every employee's mind and heart as they strive to achieve these for all students. By engaging in this process, schools will always grow to meet all their students' needs.

Also, schools should have a north star that guides them in trying times. Certain aspects can be taken off the plates of teachers, administrators, and counselors. It is important to remember what is most important when a catastrophic situation occurs. Of course, this goes back to the mission and vision; it also incorporates the aspects that have made the school unique in fulfilling these. It is okay to eliminate what is not important in order to best serve the needs of all stakeholders during exacerbating circumstances.

No matter the situation, schools should constantly be examining their systems. School leaders work with systems, and no system is self-perpetuating. Systems must be created with multiple people making the system work. Systems must also be constantly evaluated, seeing which aspects are working and which need improvement. This means that in all times, schools should have a human-centered design thinking mindset, in which improvement is cyclical. School leaders must be able to identify and define growth points, empathize and engage multiple stakeholders, ideate and brainstorm best solutions with a systems-oriented mindset, and then implement with constant revisions and refinements. By doing this, schools will not accept stagnancy, thus giving them a firm foundation in the event that another catastrophic act of nature occurs.

Schools must remember that equity is the plate, not another part of the plate. Equity ensures that all learners are properly addressed and given the best opportunities to achieve positive educational outcomes. Education of all students, regardless of background, is the cornerstone of the mission of all public schools. Not all students will need the same supports; schools must have systems in place for all learners and schools must realize that these systems will need flexibility to address the individuals within the schools. One vital part of equity is the consistent involvement of families in their child's education. The pandemic has exposed the need for more scholastic outreach to families in order to provide support and streamlined communication. Families must know what goes on within school walls and must be active agents in the education of their children.

The COVID-19 pandemic revealed many improvement points for schools. It placed schools on a trajectory to make long-term improvements through the immediate, fluid adversities that were beset upon everyone in education. Inequity is at the forefront of the conversation as the pandemic starkly revealed these. Schools must consistently engage in design thinking to address these inequities. While the pandemic revealed these growth points, it also revealed how important public schools are to our nation's cultural fabric. Schools provide basic needs; schools provide opportunities for students to form relationships with peers and caring adults; schools provide students with opportunities for growth and success; schools provide students with knowledge and skills necessary to be strong citizens in the future; schools are an epicenter for families and communities. As always, schools must improve their systems, as must the systems in which schools operate; however, schools are irreplaceable for the benefits they provide students and society at large.

REFERENCES

McAllister, J. (2018). Successful 1:1 Device Programs Help Students Get Online at Home." *EdTech*. https://edtechmagazine.com/k12/article/2018/07/.

Mitchell, Cory (2020, May 18). Serving special needs students during COVID-19: A rural educator's story. *Education Week*. https://www.edweek.org/teaching-learning/serving-special-needs-students-during-covid-19-a-rural-educators-story/2020/05.

Morita-Mullaney, T. (2019). Intersecting Leadership and English Learner Specialty: The Nexus of Creativity, Resistance, and Advocacy. In L. C. de Oliveira (Ed.), *The Handbook of TESOL in K–12*. https://doi.org/10.1002/9781119421702.ch27.

Rattermann, M. J., Angelov, A., Reddicks, T., Monk, J. (2021). Advancing health equity by addressing social determinants of health: Using health data to improve educational outcomes. *PLoS ONE* 16(3): e0247609. https://doi.org/10.1371/journal.pone.0247909.

US Department of Education (2020, March 16). *Fact sheet: Addressing the risk of COVID-19 in schools while protecting the civil rights of students*. https://www2.ed.gov/about/offices/list/ocr/docs/ocr-coronavirus-fact-sheet.pdf.

Chapter 6

The Educational Needs of Students with Chronic Illness

Kristin Wikel and Andrew M. Markelz

It is estimated that at least one of every four children in the United States has been diagnosed with a chronic illness (Berger et al., 2018). Chronic illnesses can negatively impact the life of a child or adolescent. Some children and adolescents with chronic illnesses may frequently miss school because of hospitalizations, doctors' appointments, or medical treatments. When students are absent from school, they are at risk of having low grades or may experience difficulties forming social relationships with peers. Many students with chronic illnesses may experience challenges when navigating the education environment. School absences, poor grades, and social isolation can contribute to educational challenges. Due to these factors, it is important that educators become familiar with the unique academic and social needs of students with chronic illnesses. Educating and supporting students with chronic illnesses is a professional and legal responsibility under the Individuals with Disabilities Education Act (2004). To assist educators in providing necessary supports and services, in this chapter we discuss: (a) common types of pediatric chronic illnesses; (b) educational plans, such as Section 504 plans and individualized education programs (IEPs), that may allow for students with chronic illnesses to be successful in the classroom; (c) the school reentry process; and (d) implications for educators.

CHRONIC ILLNESSES

Pediatric chronic illness is defined as an illness or impairment that is perceived to last for an extended period and requires intensive medical treatment beyond what is expected for someone of the same age (Nabors et al., 2018). Educators can conclude from portions of the chronic illness definition such as "last for an extended period of time" and "requires intensive medical treatment" that students who have been diagnosed with chronic illnesses may be frequently absent from school due to acute hospitalizations or medical treatments. Because of longevity and intensity, many types of pediatric chronic illnesses may negatively impact students' academic success. It is important, therefore, for educators to become familiar with several types of chronic illnesses and the impact these illnesses have on academics.

Chronic illnesses have historically been considered a low-incidence disability within the education field. This consideration was in part due to decreased survival rates and poor long-term medical outcomes for diagnosed children. Because medical advancements and treatments within the past few decades have significantly improved long-term outcomes for children, chronic illness is now considered a high-incidence student population category (Irwin et al., 2018). There also has been an increase in the number of children who are diagnosed with a chronic illness. For example, asthma and diabetes, two of the more common chronic illnesses, are on the rise for children (Berger et al., 2018).

Common Types of Chronic Illnesses

There are many types of chronic illnesses that impact both children and adolescents. Asthma, blood disorders, cancer, and sickle cell anemia are examples of some of the common types of chronic illness (Wikel & Markelz, 2023). Table 6.1 lists some common pediatric chronic illnesses, definitions, and implications (such as school attendance) for school success.

Asthma

Asthma is defined as a chronic inflammatory airway disease and is the most common noncommunicable chronic illness in children under the age of fourteen (Dharmage, Perret, & Custovic, 2019). Approximately six million children in the United States have been diagnosed with asthma, and more than half of the diagnosed children have had at least one or more asthma attacks per year (Centers for Disease Control, 2018). Asthma is a chronic lung disease that causes episodes of chest tightness, wheezing, and breathlessness (Zahran et al., 2018). Although asthma is a chronic illness that cannot be cured, it can be controlled through medical care and treatments. Asthma medical care and treatments consist of avoiding/reducing asthma triggers (that is, allergens and irritants) and using both asthma control medications (that is, inhaled corticosteroids) and reliever medications to prevent exacerbations (Zahran et al., 2018). Children with asthma may require access to medical care, such as emergency room visits, hospitalizations, and outpatient appointments. For example, between 2000 and 2009, 2.3 percent of all hospitalizations in patients younger than eighteen years were attributed to asthma (Hasegawa et al., 2013).

Students who have been diagnosed with asthma have an increased risk of experiencing challenges in the school setting. For example, intermittent hypoxia (that is, short episodes where there is an absence of oxygen in the body) may impact students' attention, language, learning, and memory (Mitchell et al., 2021). Also, students who have nocturnal asthma symptoms have difficulty with initiating sleep and maintaining sleep (Koinis-Mitchell et al., 2017). Sleep-related issues can negatively impact students' concentration and learning during school hours (Mitchell et al., 2021). In terms of academic achievement, students with asthma, especially asthma that is difficult to control by using medications and through the reeducation of asthma triggers, may have lower mathematical assessment scores and reading assessment scores compared to students without asthma (Mitchell et al., 2021). Finally, asthma is one of the leading causes of school absenteeism. Students with asthma miss approximately 2.3 more days of school per year than students who have not been diagnosed with asthma (Qin et al., 2021). Students with asthma who are frequently absent from school may miss important academic concepts, which can reduce academic achievement.

Cystic Fibrosis

Cystic fibrosis (CF) is a genetic disease with an incidence rate of approximately 1 in every 3,500 births in the United States (Cystic Fibrosis Foundation, n.d.). CF causes progressive and long-lasting lung infections, which limits the person's ability to breathe over time (Cystic Fibrosis Foundation, n.d.). CF is caused by genetic mutations in the cystic fibrosis transmembrane conductance regulator (CFTR) that causes the CFTR protein to not work properly. When the CFTR protein is dysfunctional, it cannot move chloride (that is, salt) to the cells' surfaces and results in the buildup of thick and sticky mucus in the body's organs. CF impacts the lungs, pancreas, and liver. In the lungs, CF causes a buildup of thick mucus that traps bacteria and results in lung infections, inflammation, and respiratory failure. CF affects the pancreas because the mucus blocks the release of digestive enzymes that the body uses to absorb key nutrients from food. In the liver, the thick mucus blocks bile ducts, which may cause liver disease.

CF symptoms include chronic coughs, wheezing or shortness of breath, very salty-tasting skin, and poor weight gain (De Boeck, 2020). Testing for CF is part of newborn screening tests that are mandatory in the United States, Canada, and many other countries (De Boeck, 2020). If a baby has a positive newborn screening test for CF, the baby is then given a sweat test that measures the amount of chloride on the skin. The sweat chloride test is the diagnostic test for CF. Because CF is a progressive disease that causes lung infections and malnutrition, early detection and treatment is very important. Although there is no cure for CF, there are many types of treatment plans available to help combat CF symptoms. CF treatments include chest physiotherapy (airway clearance techniques), nebulizer treatments, high-calorie vitamin supplements, medications, and exercise (Gathercole, 2019). Although many CF treatments can be done at home, children with CF may require hospitalizations to treat CF exacerbations (Gathercole, 2019).

Students with CF benefit from accommodations in the school setting. Although CF is not linked to decreases in cognition or learning disabilities, many students with CF struggle in school. The majority of the academic challenges that students with CF encounter can be attributed to school absences (Gathercole, 2019). Also, because students with CF may be frequently absent from school, they are more likely to feel disconnected with their peers. Finally, school personnel need to be careful placing students with CF in the same classrooms. Although CF is not contagious, students with CF (nonfamily members) are more likely to transmit germs between each other when they are in close proximity (Cystic Fibrosis Foundation, n.d.). Whenever there are two or more students (nonfamily members) with CF in the same school, the Cystic Fibrosis Foundation recommends that the students with CF be placed in separate classrooms, be assigned different times to use general common areas (that is, cafeterias, gyms, etc.), take their medications in different school locations, do not share school materials, and wear masks at all times.

Diabetes

Diabetes is a very common chronic illness in children. Approximately 200,000 school-aged children have been diagnosed with diabetes, and the number of school aged children with diabetes continues to increase (Jackson et al., 2015). There are two types of diabetes: type 1 and type 2. In type 1 diabetes, the most common form of diabetes in children, the body does not produce insulin. Insulin is a hormone that is used to transport glucose (that is, blood sugar) from the bloodstream to the body's cells. Type 2 diabetes, the most common form of diabetes in adults, causes the body to not use insulin properly. Symptoms of diabetes include frequent urination, extreme thirst, fatigue, blurry vision, increase in hunger, and cuts or bruises that heal slowly (American Diabetes Association, 2022).

There are several ways that diabetes is diagnosed. The three most common diagnostic tests are the A1C test, the fasting plasma glucose test, and the oral glucose tolerance test. The A1C test measures a person's average blood glucose for the past two to three months, the fasting plasma glucose test measures fasting blood glucose levels, and the oral glucose tolerance test is a two-hour test that measures the body's blood glucose levels before and after a sweet drink is given (American Diabetes Association, 2022). Treatment of diabetes consists of checking blood glucose levels frequently, taking insulin or other medications, following a healthy meal plan, and engaging in regular exercise. Insulin can be delivered through an insulin infusion pump or through multiple daily injections (Jackson et al., 2015). Diabetic ketoacidosis (DKA) is a very serious complication for individuals with type 1 diabetes. DKA occurs when the body does not have enough insulin. Because insulin helps to transfer glucose from the blood to the cells, when there is not enough insulin the cells begin to burn fat to use for energy. Ketones are the acids that build up in the blood as a result of the cells burning fat. Excess ketones in a person's body causes the body to go into shock, which can result in seizures, coma, and even death (American Diabetes Association, 2022).

Because students with diabetes are at risk for serious medical complications, it is important that individualized diabetes medical management plans (DMMP) are written that detail the student's unique medical needs. Depending on the student's specific diabetes needs, the DMMP may include information regarding blood glucose monitoring, insulin administration, meals and snacks, treatment of hypoglycemia (low blood glucose) and hyperglycemia (high blood glucose), checking for ketones, and emergency plans in the event of a school emergency (that is, school evacuations or school lockdowns; Jackson et al., 2015). Students with diabetes may also have attention difficulties and memory issues, especially in the event of high or low blood glucose levels. Because diabetes is a chronic life-long illness, students with diabetes benefit from Section 504 plans and/or special education and related services.

Leukemia

Leukemia, a type of blood cancer, is the most common cancer in children, and it accounts for approximately 30 percent of all pediatric cancer diagnoses (Kaplan, 2019). There are three distinct types of leukemia: acute lymphoblastic leukemia (ALL), acute myelogenous leukemia (AML), and chronic myelogenous leukemia (CML). ALL is the most common type of leukemia, with 80 percent of all leukemia cases classified as ALL (Kaplan, 2019). Symptoms of leukemia can include bruising, fevers, joint or bone pain, and fatigue (Kaplan, 2019). Leukemia is diagnosed through a bone marrow aspirate. The bone marrow aspirate is used to determine the extent to which the bone marrow has been replaced by leukemic blasts. Bone marrow is the tissues located inside bones and produces red blood cells, platelets, and white blood cells. Red blood cells carry oxygen through the body, white blood cells help the body fight off infections, and platelets help with blood clotting. Many children with leukemia have high white blood cell counts; however, most of the white blood cells are not functioning properly because they have been replaced by leukemic cells (Kaplan, 2019).

Due to advancements in medicine and medical treatments, childhood leukemia has a high survival rate. For example, in the 1960s the survival rate of leukemia in children was approximately 10 percent, and in 2021, the survival rate was 90 percent (Mavrea et al., 2021). Leukemia is treated by chemotherapy, which is used to stop the growth of cancer cells. Chemotherapy can be administered in many ways. Some of the common types of chemotherapy administration are orally (pills or liquids), topically (cream that is rubbed on the skin), through injections, intrathecal (injected into the tissues), intraperitoneal (injected into the peritoneal cavity), or intra-arterial (injected into the arteries).

Children who are undergoing treatment for leukemia and children who are leukemia survivors have many physical, emotional, and cognitive needs that may impact their education. Chemotherapy can have an adverse effect on neurocognitive development, which results in decreased attention, impacted learning abilities, and lower cognition (Mavrea et al., 2021). Also, children with leukemia are likely to be absent from school for long periods of time due to medical treatments. School absences can impact learning and socialization for students with leukemia. Due to their school absences and learning difficulties, students with leukemia are more likely to repeat grades in school than their peers without cancer (Mavrea et al., 2021). Because of the increased risk of learning, attention, and socialization difficulties, students with leukemia benefit from either special education and related services or accommodations provided under Section 504 plans.

Chronic Illness Comorbidities

Psychological disorders are one of the most prevalent comorbid disorders found in children and adolescents with chronic illnesses. Approximately 60 percent of youth with chronic illness also have been diagnosed with a psychological disorder as compared with 10 percent to 20 percent of the pediatric population (Lau et al., 2020). Many times, students with chronic illness experience a sense of uncertainty about the future. They often worry about missed school time and social isolation due to illness and hospitalization. These emotional factors may lead to psychological distress for students with chronic illness. It is important to remember that pediatric chronic illnesses do not operate in silos. There is a high probability that comorbidity exists, meaning secondary and tertiary conditions are present (either medically, psychologically, or both).

Table 6.1. Significant Chronic Illnesses: Definitions and Impact on Education

Chronic Illness	Definition	Academic and/or Social Needs	Average School Year Absences
Asthma	Chronic lung disease with periods of acute breathing problems including wheezing, coughing, chest tightness, or shortness of breath.	Fatigue can cause anxiety and confusion.	12–36 days
Cancer: Leukemia	Leukemia is a fast-growing cancer of white blood cells.	Fatigue, increased risk for infections, loss of appetite, hair loss, attention difficulties.	25–80 days, depending on specific cancer diagnosis and treatment plan
Cystic Fibrosis (CF)	CF is a genetic disease that causes persistent lung infections and reduces the ability to breathe over time. There is no cure for the disease.	Stunted height and weight growth, overall pulmonary difficulties, reduction in appetite, academic and social difficulties due to increased absences.	19.5 days
Cardiac Conditions (for example, congenital heart defects [CHD])	CHD: holes in the heart, obstructed blood flow, abnormal blood vessels, heart valve abnormalities, an underdeveloped heart, and combination of defects.	Some children with CHD have early delays in development, which makes early assessment and support vitally important.	10 or more days per year
Diabetes	This is a condition that causes a shortage of insulin, a hormone that allows sugar to enter the body's cells and to be converted into energy.	Verbal IQ, visuospatial/nonverbal functioning, memory, attention issues, especially if there is a high prevalence of seizures, unconsciousness.	14 days
Juvenile Idiopathic Arthritis (JIA)	JIA is an inflammation of joints (ages sixteen or younger). An autoimmune disorder that causes periodic painful flares.	Children with JIA can experience a decrease in concentration, academic difficulties due to heightened absences, and significant mood swings.	15 days
Sickle Cell Anemia (SCA)	SCA is an inherited blood disorder, causes periodic episodes of severe pain.	Difficulties with verbal abilities, processing, attention, and memory. Periodic pain crises increase risk for missing school days.	20 days

Note: Information adapted from American Cancer Society, Inc. (2010); National Heart, Lung, and Blood Inst. (Frommer, 1991); Shaw & McCabe (2008); Taras & Potts-Datema (2005).

EDUCATIONAL IMPLICATIONS FOR STUDENTS WITH CHRONIC ILLNESSES

Individuals with Disabilities Education Act (2004)

The Individuals with Disabilities Education Act (IDEA, 2004) is the nation's special education legislation that enables students with disabilities to receive special education and related services based on their individualized needs. In order to receive special education services, students must have a qualifying disability (or disabilities), and the disability must adversely impact the students' education (Markelz & Bateman, 2022). Students suspected of a disability must first undergo special education evaluations, and then a multidisciplinary team meets to review the evaluations and determine special education eligibility. If a student is found eligible for special education and related services, the team meets to write the IEP. The student and the student's parents are integral members of the IEP team, and they should be active members of the IEP process. IDEA (2004) has thirteen eligible disability categories:

- Autism
- Deaf-blindness
- Deafness
- Hearing impairment
- Intellectual disability
- Multiple disabilities
- Orthopedic impairments
- Other health impairments
- Emotional disturbance
- Specific learning disability
- Speech or language impairment
- Traumatic brain injury
- Visual impairment or blindness

If a chronic illness adversely impacts a student's education, the student may benefit from special education and related services. Chronic illnesses are usually identified as an IEP eligible disability under the other health impairments (OHI) category. IDEA (2004) defines OHI as having limited strength, alertness, or vitality, including heightened or limited alertness to the educational environment that is due to acute or chronic health problems, and adversely affects the student's educational performance. Many chronic illnesses, such as leukemia, sickle cell, cystic fibrosis, etc., may adversely impact students' educational performances and impact students' strength, alertness, and vitality in the school setting.

Free appropriate public education (FAPE) is an important factor of IDEA legislation. "Free education" means all special education and related services are provided at no cost to families (Markelz & Bateman, 2022). "Public education" means students who are eligible for special education services can receive preschool, elementary, and secondary education in state accredited public schools (Markelz & Bateman, 2022). "Appropriate education" is defined as education services that are appropriate for the students' individualized needs (Markelz & Bateman, 2022). To meet the definition of appropriate, the US Supreme Court in *Endrew F. v. Douglas County School District* (2017) clarified a two-part test that can be used in determining the appropriateness of a student's special education services. The two-part test addresses both the procedural and substantive requirements of IDEA (2004). The two-part test asks:

1. Has the school district complied with the procedures of the IDEA?
2. Is the IEP reasonably calculated to enable the student to make appropriate progress in light of the student's circumstances?

An important factor of FAPE is that the student's special education and related services are individualized to meet the student's specific needs. When evaluating FAPE for students with chronic illness who are found eligible for special education and related services, IEP teams should consider how the student's medical condition impacts the student's education. Some factors to consider are disease severity and condition, student's response to treatment, how seasons impact the illness, and the potential risk of exacerbations (that is, flareups) of the illness.

Rehabilitation Act of 1973: Section 504

The Rehabilitation Act of 1973 is a civil rights legislation that protects individuals with disabilities from discrimination. The Office for Civil Rights (OCR) is responsible for enforcing Section 504 regulations in all programs that receive federal financial assistance (Office for Civil Rights, 2020). Public schools, higher education institutions, and other state and local education agencies receive federal financial assistance, therefore they must adhere to Section 504 regulations. Section 504 provisions specify that school districts are required to provide FAPE to qualifying students with disabilities, regardless of disease severity or condition (Office for Civil Rights, 2020). Also, FAPE under Section 504 consists of special education and related services that are designed to meet the student's specific needs as adequately as the needs of the student's nondisabled peers (Office for Civil Rights, 2020).

Section 504 regulations are enforced by the OCR, and IDEA (2004) regulations are enforced by the Office of Special Education and Rehabilitative Services. IDEA (2004) funds special education, and each state education agency is required to monitor IDEA's regulations along with distributing IDEA's federal funds to schools. Section 504 laws do not provide any federal funding (Office for Civil Rights, 2020).

To qualify for Section 504 protections, a student must be determined to (a) have a physical and/or mental impairment that limits one or more major life activities; or (b) have record of such impairments; or (c) be regarded as having such impairments (Office for Civil Rights, 2020). Section 504 lists some conditions that may constitute physical or mental impairments, however the provision does not have an exhaustive list of specific conditions because of difficulty ensuring a comprehensive list. Thinking, learning, reading, concentration, etc. (for example, aspects of education) are some examples of "major life activities" under Section 504.

In order to be eligible for Section 504 provisions, students must first undergo an evaluation to determine if the student's physical or mental impairment impacts education. According to Section 504 regulations, a medical diagnosis does not automatically qualify students for services under Section 504 (Office for Civil Rights, 2020). Although a medical diagnosis may be considered as part of the student's Section 504 evaluation, the student's medical condition must substantially limit learning or other aspects of education. Students with chronic illnesses may qualify for Section 504 services if they meet Section 504's definition on physical and mental impairments substantially impacting one or more life activities.

Accommodations and Modifications

Accommodations and modifications are words that are commonly used during the development of IEPs or Section 504 plans. Although students with chronic illnesses benefit from accommodations and modifications, these words have vastly different meanings. Accommodations are adaptations made to the academic curriculum that compensate for students' areas of need without modifying the curriculum (Markelz & Bateman, 2022). In other words, accommodations change *how* students learn the curriculum. Modifications are adaptations made to the curriculum that compensate for students' weaknesses by changing the curriculum or academic standards (Markelz & Bateman, 2022). Modifications change *what* students learn. For example, a graphic organizer provided to students to assist with essay writing is an accommodation that can compensate for organizational or executive functioning deficits. An essay writing modification for students with organizational or executive functioning deficits may include substituting the essay assignment with an alternative task.

Many students with chronic illnesses benefit from accommodations and modifications in the school setting. Specific accommodations and modifications should be discussed during the student's IEP or Section 504 plan meeting. Accommodations and modifications should be specific to the student's individual learning needs and need to be included in the student's IEP or Section 504 plan. For example, some students with chronic illnesses fatigue with extensive writing or typing tasks and may benefit from having access to word prediction or text to speech software. Other students with chronic illnesses may have difficulty with attention to academic tasks and may benefit from learning breaks or access to fidgets. Table 6.2 lists examples of accommodations and modifications for students with chronic illnesses.

Table 6.2. Examples of Accommodations and Modifications

Accommodations	Modifications
Learning Environment	
Adapted physical education	Excused from physical education
Extra time during passing periods or between classes	
Half-day school schedule, late arrival to school, or early dismissal from school	
Preferential seating	
Two sets of classroom textbooks: one set kept at home and one set kept at school	
Use of elevator	
Use of appropriate fidgets	
Classroom Materials and Assignments	
Allow different options to respond	Excused from assignments
Use of calculators	Providing assignments at students' instructional level, not grade level
Materials in large print	
Extended time to complete assignments	Alternative assignments with different requirements
Instructions provided in multiple modalities	Learning different material (that is, different vocabulary words or math concepts)
Use of audio books or screen readers	Reword books, passages, etc., into simpler language
Use of scribe or other dictation technology	Modify curriculum to focus on key concepts and/or vocabulary
Extra time to complete tests	Modify tests to assess a few key concepts
Use of graphic organizers, note outlines, etc.	Alternative grading system (that is, pass/fail)

School Attendance

Educational attainment is one of the strongest predictors of an individual's quality of life and overall health outcomes (Low & Low, 2006). Students must be present and engaged within the school environment to learn. Many students who are chronically absent from school may not have the opportunity to be actively engaged in the learning process and form positive peer relationships.

Chronic absenteeism refers to the number of days students are absent from school. Unexcused absences, excused absences, and absences related to discipline reasons are included in the chronic absenteeism measurement (Rafa, 2017). The US Department of Education (USDOE) and the OCR define chronic absenteeism as missing fifteen or more days of school in a year (Office for Civil Rights & US Department of Education, 2016). Some states and local districts measure chronic absenteeism as a percentage of days missed. In these situations, being absent 10 percent (eighteen days) of school is considered being chronically absent (Attendance Works & Everyone Graduates Center, 2016). According to the OCR and USDOE, over seven million students, or 16 percent of the total student population, missed fifteen or more days of school during the 2015–2016 school year.

There are many long-term academic consequences for the more than seven million US students who miss more than fifteen days of school in a year. For example, students who are chronically absent in kindergarten have an increased risk of being retained in the third grade (Ginsburg, Jordan, & Chang, 2014). The increased risk for retention at third grade is due to reduced academic achievement scores and the difficulty with mastery of reading and math concepts. As students move from elementary school to middle school, the academic material increases in its complexity. When students are chronically absent from middle school, they experience many challenges that extend into high school. Middle school attendance and overall GPA are the two most important factors that predict how well students will do in high school (Allensworth et al., 2014).

Students who are chronically absent from high school experience higher rates of high school dropout, decreased health outcomes, and higher rates of incarceration. Academic performance in ninth grade is the most important predictor of high school graduation (Balfanz & Byrnes, 2012). There is a strong correlation between school attendance and academic performance. For example, a research study on school attendance in high school found that students who had high test scores but missed two or more weeks of school during a semester were more likely to fail than peers who perform poorly on tests but had good attendance (Allensworth & Easton, 2007).

High School Graduation

Students who drop out of school prior to graduation also have an increased likelihood of being incarcerated or becoming involved with the legal systems. A juvenile justice review of Rhode Island and New York City showed that at least 75 percent of students who were involved within the juvenile justice system have histories of chronic absenteeism (Balfanz & Byrnes, 2012). When students experience chronic absences or truancy during childhood, the probability that the students will experience homelessness, poverty, engagement in criminal activity, and substance abuse increased during adulthood (Bennett et al., 2018).

Also, there are substantial societal costs when students drop out of high school. When an individual has a history of chronic absenteeism or truancy and drops out of high school, society will pay as much as $800,000 over the course of the individual's lifetime (Lochmiller, 2013). Individuals who drop out of high school earn less, pay less in income taxes, and incur higher juvenile and/or adult criminal justice costs than individuals who graduate high school (Lochmiller, 2013). Students who are chronically absent or truant cost schools extra money in providing extra support services such as counseling, remediation sessions, and before/after school services. Finally, students who have excessive absences can ultimately cause schools to lose out on education funds that are tied to student attendance. Because most schools receive funding based upon average daily membership rates, when students are chronically absent, the schools receive less funding (Lochmiller, 2013).

As described in the previous sections of this chapter, there are many medical, educational, social/emotional, and financial costs associated with the education of students with chronic illnesses. To alleviate some of these challenges, researchers have examined strategies and programs to assist medical and educational communities in coordinating necessary supports to provide appropriate educational service to this population of students.

SCHOOL REENTRY

School reentry is the academic and social reintegration of students back in the school setting after prolonged periods of absences. School reentry involves coordinated efforts among the student with chronic illness, the student's family, school personnel, and medical professionals. Some medical systems, such as pediatric hospitals, rehabilitation facilities, and behavioral health centers, employ school liaisons who facilitate students' school reintegration. School liaisons typically have backgrounds in education, nursing, or social work, and they help identify appropriate school accommodations that will benefit students with chronic illnesses upon their return to school. The Hospital Educator and Academic Liaison (HEAL) Association is a national organization that is dedicated to school liaisons and other hospital-based educational professionals (https://www.healassociation.org).

School reentry programs should focus on the two important parts of education: academic achievement and social skills. Many academic concepts are taught in sequential order, and if students with chronic illnesses are frequently absent from school, they are at risk for lower academic achievement. Education is also a highly social function where students have many opportunities, especially in the early grades, to learn and practice their social skills. Students with chronic illnesses may have fewer opportunities to interact with their peers because their illnesses can cause them to be frequently absent from school. There are three types of school reentry programs: (a) school personnel–focused reentry programs, (b) peer-focused reentry programs, and (c) student-focused reentry programs (Wikel & Markelz, 2023). Although empirical research regarding the effectiveness of school reentry programs is limited, school reentry programs that have been shown to be effective have focused on both academic achievement and social skills of students with chronic illnesses (Wikel & Markelz, 2023).

School Personnel Reentry Programs

School personnel programs are types of reentry programs that provide education on chronic illnesses to school employees. Many school staff feel unprepared to meet the academic and social needs of students with chronic illnesses (Wikel & Markelz, 2023). School personnel reentry programs usually consist of providing printed or web-based education materials on chronic illnesses to school personnel. Through the use of multimedia tools, such as web-based modules, school personnel reentry programs can educate large audiences (that is, entire school corporations) on chronic illnesses.

The aims of school personnel reentry programs are to increase school employees' knowledge on chronic illness, which increases the likelihood that school employees will have a greater understanding of education challenges faced by students with chronic illnesses. Although there are many benefits of school personnel reentry programs (that is, increasing chronic illness knowledge), there are some disadvantages to using this type of program. Research on school personnel reentry programs found a decrease over time in educator use of the multimedia tools on chronic illness (Wikel & Markelz, 2023). Also, there is little research on the type of chronic illness content that is most beneficial in increasing school personnel's knowledge on chronic illnesses. Finally, school personnel programs have shown to increase educator knowledge and confidence on chronic illness; however, further investigation is needed to identify if educators' knowledge on chronic illnesses translates to positive social and academic outcomes for students with chronic illnesses.

Peer Support Reentry Programs

Peer support reentry programs are another type of school reentry program that provides age-appropriate chronic illness information to school-age students. Peer support reentry programs target the social aspect of school. Students with chronic illnesses may be frequently absent from school and are at a high risk for peer victimization and peer rejection (Runions et al., 2020). By providing chronic illness education to peers, peer support reentry programs may reduce the stigmatization surrounding students with chronic illness. Given that knowledge and attitudes can be used as a predictor of behavior (Ajzen, 1980; Sussman & Gifford, 2019), it is understandable that peer support reentry programs can increase peers' knowledge and understanding of chronic illnesses.

Although peer support reentry programs target students with chronic illnesses, further research is needed to determine if these types of programs positively impact the school reentry process for students with chronic illnesses. For example, many students with cystic fibrosis may present with a cough that is associated with the disease; however, for some peers, the cough may be perceived as the students being unwell or contagious (Runions et al., 2020). The student with cystic fibrosis may be ostracized by their peers, which decreases the student's sense of school belonging. By providing chronic illness information to peers, these reentry programs can increase the likelihood of peers forming social relationships with students who have been diagnosed with chronic illnesses. Further research is needed on peer-focused reentry programs to identify if changes in peers' attitudes and beliefs in chronic illnesses also changes peers' behaviors toward students with chronic illnesses.

Student-Focused Reentry Programs

Student-focused reentry programs are defined as comprehensive school reentry programs that focus on the individualized needs of students with chronic illnesses. Because student-focused reentry programs are individualized to the students' unique needs, these programs are able to consider the students' specific illnesses and medical treatments that may impact academic achievement and social emotional outcomes. In two separate research studies on student-focused reentry programs (see Colbert et al., 2020; Koontz et al.,

2004), it was found that students who participated in these reentry programs demonstrated an increase in chronic illness knowledge and showed improvements in school attendance and positive social emotional growth.

Comprehensive school reentry programs are typically initiated by hospital-based school liaisons who work with students with chronic illnesses and their families to identify school reentry needs that are specific to the student. Although comprehensive school reentry programs have been shown to improve educational outcomes for students with chronic illnesses, there are barriers to implementing these programs. One barrier is the high costs medical facilities incur from implementing school reentry programs and salaries of educational liaisons who are devoted to this work. Because school reentry programs are non-revenue-generating programs, these programs may be cost prohibitive to the medical facilities that employ school liaisons. Finally, large pediatric facilities support many patients, which ultimately may translate to hospital liaisons triaging school reentry needs so that only a portion of students with chronic illnesses receive reentry services.

One possible solution to overcome cost-prohibitive barriers is through the use of telemedicine practices to virtually connect with patients, their families, school personnel, and peers. Many families and schools are familiar with various video conferencing software platforms, so telemedicine practices may be easy to implement. By using telemedicine or other video conferencing platforms, school liaisons may be able to increase their caseloads as they no longer will need to travel to schools to provide in-person reentry sessions.

CHRONIC ILLNESS IMPLICATIONS FOR EDUCATORS

Medical advancements have increased the survival rates of chronic illnesses and have allowed many students with chronic illnesses to attend school with education and nursing support. Because the prevalence of students with chronic illnesses who are attending school has risen, it is important that special education teachers and general education teachers are able to provide appropriate education supports to meet the needs of students with chronic illnesses.

Partnerships with School Nurses

Many students with chronic illnesses need health plans at school. Therefore, school nurse and teacher partnerships are very important to approach a student's individual medical needs from a holistic view. For example, students with asthma may need access to emergency medications in the event of asthma exacerbation at school. School nurses can provide asthma education to teachers, which can include environmental factors that may increase the likelihood of asthma exacerbation. At the same time, school nurses may be able to provide peer students education on chronic illnesses to alleviate stigmatism. Unfortunately for many school districts, however, there are significant shortages in school nurse availability (Vestel, 2021). Across the United States at least 25 percent of schools have no nurse and 35 percent have only a part-time nurse (Willgerodt et al., 2018).

Medical/Educational/Family Partnerships

Many students with chronic illnesses are frequently absent from school to attend medical appointments, acute hospitalizations, or to receive medical treatments. Because students with chronic illnesses receive medical care from a variety of different medical providers, it is important that families, schools, and medical teams collaborate and exchange information relating to the students' treatment plans. Although there are not medical/educational/family collaboration standards, a growing amount of research has identified a set of best collaboration practices (Schilling & Getch, 2017). The best practices are: (a) input from schools, families, and medical professionals involved in the student's care; (b) identification of the student's learning and social-emotional needs in relation to the chronic illness; (c) discussion of any physical limitations that are attributed to the student's chronic illness; and (d) plans for reviewing the student's academic and social-emotional learning (Schilling & Getch, 2017).

Information Sharing

Information sharing is a valuable tool in medical/educational/family partnerships. When establishing communication networks, educator professionals and medical providers must adhere to specific patient/student privacy laws that protect against releasing medical or education information without parental consent. The Health Insurance Portability and Accountability Act of 1996 (HIPAA) is a federal law that protects sensitive health information from being disclosed without the patient's consent or legal caregiver's consent (Centers for Disease Control and Prevention, 2022b). Another privacy law, the Family Educational Rights and Privacy Act (FERPA) was enacted in 1974 and protects the privacy of student education records (Centers for Disease Control and Prevention, 2022a). FERPA applies to all public or private elementary, secondary, and postsecondary schools and prohibits the disclosure of personally identifiable education records (Centers for Disease Control and Prevention, 2022a). Prior to exchanging medical or educational information, school personnel and medical providers need to obtain written consent from the student's legal caregivers. Also, school personnel and medical providers need to ensure that medical/education information is kept in secure locations and that only information that is pertinent to the student's academic performance or medical care is exchanged.

Communication on Progress

After school personnel and medical providers obtain legal consent from the students' parents or legal guardians, plans for how and when communication between families, schools, and medical professionals should be established. There are many factors that should be considered, such as medical treatment phases, medication side effects, and upcoming surgeries or procedures when developing communication plans. For example, school personnel, families, and medical providers may want to meet once per month to discuss the educational implications for a student with leukemia who is receiving monthly chemotherapy. Families, school personnel, and medical providers may meet to update a health plan for a student with asthma after the student experienced an asthma exacerbation.

Focus on the Individual Needs of Students with Chronic Illnesses

When developing education plans for students with chronic illnesses, general education and special education teachers, school administrators, and school nurses should consider how the student's unique medical condition impacts the student's academic performance and peer relationships. Educators should be attentive to the individual needs of students with chronic illnesses and adjust as necessary to benefit their students. General education and special education teachers can use progress monitoring techniques to collect data individualized to the student. Data on the student's academic performance and social relationships can be used to update a student's health plan, Section 504 plan, or IEP.

CONCLUSION

Students with chronic illnesses are a diverse population of learners. Although asthma is the most prevalent chronic illness in children, there are many types of chronic illnesses that may impact a student's school attendance, academic achievement, and peer relationships. Many students with chronic illnesses benefit from formalized education plans such as IEPs, Section 504 plans, or health plans. Because students with chronic illnesses may be frequently absent from school, school reentry programs that are student focused and consider the individual needs of the student will aid in the transition back to school settings. Partnerships between families, school personnel, and medical professionals that focus on communication and collaboration are critical to the successful education of students with chronic illnesses.

REFERENCES

Ajzen, I. (1980). *Understanding the attitudes and predicting social behavior.* Englewood Cliffs, NJ: Prentice-Hall.

Allensworth, E. M., & Easton, J. Q. (2007). What matters for staying on-track and graduating in Chicago public high schools: A close look at course grades, failures, and attendance in the freshman year (ED498350). ERIC. https://eric.ed.gov/?id=ED498350.

Allensworth, E. M., Gwynne, J. A., Moore, P., & de la Torre, M. (2014). *Five key findings for middle grades: From looking forward to high school and college.* University of Chicago Consortium on Chicago School Research. https://www.attendanceworks.org/wp-content/uploads/2017/09/5-Key-Findings-MG-Final.pdf.

American Cancer Society, Inc. (2020). When your child has cancer. https://www.cancer.org/treatment/children-and-cancer/when-your-child-has-cancer.html.

American Diabetes Association (2022). Diabetes overview. https://www.diabetes.org/diabetes.

Balfanz, R., & Byrnes, V. (2012). The importance of being in school: A report on absenteeism in the nation's public schools. *The Education Digest, 78*(4), 1–46.

Bennett, S., Mazerolle, L., Antrobus, E., Eggins, E., & Piquero, A. R. (2018). Truancy intervention reduces crime: Results from a randomized field trial. *Justice Quarterly, 35*(2), 309–29. https://doi.org/10.1080/07418825.2017.1313440.

Berger, C., Valenzuela, J., Tsikis, J., & Fletcher, C. (2018). School professionals' knowledge and beliefs about youth with chronic illness. *The Journal of School Health, 88*(8), 615–23.

Bills, S. E., Schatz, J., Hardy, S. J., & Reinman, L. (2020). Social-environmental factors and cognitive and behavioral functioning in pediatric sickle cell disease. *Child Neuropsychology, 26*(1), 83–99.

Centers for Disease Control and Prevention (2018). Asthma in children. https://www.cdc.gov/vitalsigns/childhood-asthma.

Centers for Disease Control and Prevention (2022a). Family educational rights and privacy act (FERPA). https://www.cdc.gov/phlp/publications/topic/ferpa.html.

Centers for Disease Control and Prevention (2022b). Health insurance portability and accountability act of 1996 (HIPAA). https://www.cdc.gov/phlp/publications/topic/hipaa.html.

Colbert, A. M., Edlynn, E., Mueller, V., Ariefdjohan, M., & Lindwall, J. (2020). Evaluating health-related quality of life and school attendance in a multidisciplinary school program for youth with significant medical needs. *Journal of Clinical Psychology in Medical Settings, 27*, 416–28. https://doi.org/10.1007/s10880-019-09675-7.

Cystic Fibrosis Foundation (n.d.). A teacher's guide to cystic fibrosis. https://www.cff.org/intro-cf/teachers-guide-cystic-fibrosis.

De Boeck, K. (2020). Cystic fibrosis in the year 2020: A disease with a new face. *Acta Paediatrica, 109*(5), 893–99. https://doi.org/10.1111/apa.15155.

Dharmage, S. C., Perret, J. L., & Custovic, A. (2019). Epidemiology of asthma in children and adults. *Frontiers in Pediatrics, 7*, 1–15. https://doi.org/10.3389/fped.2019.00246.

Endrew F. v. Douglas County School District, 137 S. Ct. 988 (2017).

Essawy, M. A., Sharkawy, A. E., Shabbani, Z. A., & Reda, A. (2018). Quality of life of children with sickle cell anemia. *Journal of Nursing and Health Science, 7*(2), 29–39.

Frommer, P. L. (1991). An overview of the National Heart, Lung, and Blood Institute Artificial Heart Program. In Akutsu, T., et al. *Artificial Heart 3*. Springer, Tokyo. https://doi.org/10.1007/978-4-431-68126-7_1.

Gathercole, K. (2019). Managing cystic fibrosis alongside children's schooling: Family, nurse and teacher perspectives. *Journal of Child Health Care, 23*(3), 425–36. https://doi.org/10.1177/1367493518814930.

Ginsburg, A., Jordan, P., & Chang, H. (2014). Absences add up: How school attendance influences student success. Attendance Works. https://www.attendanceworks.org/wp-content/uploads/2017/05/Absenses-Add-Up_September-3rd-2014.pdf.

Ginsburg, G. S., Becker, E. M., Keeton, C. P., Sakolsky, D., Piacentini, J., Albano, A. M., Compton, S. N., Iyengar, S., Sullivan, K., Caporino, N., Peris, T., Birmaher, B., Rynn, M., March, J., Kendall, P. C. (2014). Naturalistic follow-up of youths treated for pediatric anxiety disorders. *JAMA Psychiatry* 71(3):310–18. doi: 10.1001/jamapsychiatry.2013.4186. PMID: 24477837; PMCID: PMC3969570.

Hasegawa, K., Tsugawa, Y., Brown, D. F. M., & Camargo, C. A. (2013). Childhood asthma hospitalizations in the United States, 2000–2009. *The Journal of Pediatrics, 163*(4), 1127–33. https://doi.org/10.1016/j.jpeds.2013.05.002.

Individuals with Disabilities Education Improvement Act (IDEA) of 2004, Pub. L. No. 108-446, U.S.C. § 1400 *et seq.* (2004).

Irwin, M. K., Elam, M., Merianos, A., Nabors, L., & Murphy, C. (2018). Training and preparedness to meet the needs of students with a chronic health condition in the school setting: An examination of teacher preparation programming in the United States. *Physical Disabilities: Education and Related Services, 37*(2), 34–59. https://doi.org/10.14434/pders.v37i2.26254.

Jackson, C. C., Albanese-O'Neil, A., Butler, K. L., Chiang, J. L., Deeb, L. C., Hathaway, K., Kraus, E., Weissberg-Benchell, J., Yatvin, A. L., & Siminerio, L. M. (2015). Diabetes care in the school setting: A position statement of the American Diabetes Association. *Diabetes Care, 38*(10), 1958–63. https://doi.org/10.2337/dc15-1418.

Kaplan, J. A. (2019). Leukemia in children. *Pediatrics in Review, 40*(7), 319–31. https://doi.org/10.1542/pir.2018-0192.

Koinis-Mitchell, D., Kopel, S. J., Seifer, R., LeBourgeois, M., McQuaid, E. L., Esteban, C. A., Boergers, J., Nassau, J., Farrow, M., Fritz, G. K., & Klein, R. B. (2017). Asthma-related lung function, sleep quality, and sleep duration in urban children. *Sleep Health, 3*(3), 148–56. https://doi.org/10.1016/j.sleh.2017.03.008.

Koontz, K., Short, A. D., Kalinyak, K., & Noll, R. B. (2004). A randomized, controlled pilot trial of a school intervention for children with sickle cell anemia. *Journal of Pediatric Psychology, 29*(1), 7–17. https://doi.org/10.1093/jpepsy/jsh002.

Lau, N., Waldbaum, S., Parigoris, R., O'Daffer, A., Walsh, C., Colt, S. F., Yi-Frazier, J. P., Palermo, T. M., McCauley, E., & Rosenberg, A. R. (2020). eHealth and mHealth psychosocial interventions for youths with chronic illness: Systematic review. *JMIR Pediatric Parent, 3*(2), e22329.

Lochmiller, C. R. (2013). *Improving student attendance in Indiana's schools: Synthesis of existing research related to student absenteeism and effective, research-based interventions.* Center for Evaluation & Education Policy.

Low, B. J., & Low, M. D. (2006). Education and education policy as social determinant of health. *AMA Journal of Ethics, 8*(11), 756–61.

Markelz, A. M., & Bateman, D. F. (2022). *The essentials of special education law.* Roman & Littlefield.

Mavrea, K., Efthymiou, V., Katsibardi, K., Tsarouhas, K., Kanaka-Gantenbein, C., Spandidos, D., Chrousos, G., Kattamis, A., & Bacopoulou, F. (2021). Cognitive function of children and adolescent survivors of acute lymphoblastic leukemia: A meta-analysis. *Oncology Letters, 21*(4), 1–9. https://doi.org/10.3892/ol.2021.12523.

Mitchell, R. J., McMaugh, A., Homaira, N., Reidar, P. L., Badgery-Parker, T., & Camerson, C. M. (2021). The impact of childhood asthma on academic performance: A matched population-based cohort study. *Clinical & Experimental Allergy, 52*(2), 286–96. https://doi.org/10.1111/cea.14022.

Nabors, L., Cunningham, J. F., Lang, M., Wood, K., Southwick, S., & Stough, C. O. (2018). Family coping during hospitalization of children with chronic illness. *Journal of Child and Family Studies, 27*(5), 1482–91. https://doi.org/10.1007/s10826-017-0986-.

Office for Civil Rights (2020). Protection students with disabilities. https://www2.ed.gov/about/offices/list/ocr/504faq.html.

Office for Civil Rights & US Department of Education (2016). *Chronic absenteeism in the nation's schools: A hidden crisis.* https://www.2.ed.gov/datastory/chronicabsenteeism.html.

Qin, X., Zahran, H. S., Leon-Nguyen, M., Kilmer, G., Collins, P., Welch, P., & Malilay, J. (2021). Trends in asthma-related school health policies and practices in the US states. *Journal of School Health, 92*(3), 252–60. https://doi.org/10.1111/josh.13124.

Rafa, A. (2017). *Chronic absenteeism: A key indicator for student success.* Education Commission for the States. https://www.ecs.org.

Runions, K., Vithiatharan, R., Hancock, K., Lin, A., Brennan-Jones, C. B., Gray, C., & Payne, D. (2020). Chronic health conditions, mental health and the school: A narrative review. *Health Education Journal, 79*(4), 471–83. https://doi.org/10.1177/0017896919890898.

Schilling, E. J., & Getch, Y. Q. (2017). School reentry services for students with chronic health conditions: An examination of regional practices. *Psychology in the Schools, 55,* 1027–40. https://doi.org/10.1002/pits.22154.

Shaw, S. R., & McCabe, P. C. (2008). Hospital-to-school transition for children with chronic illness: Meeting the new challenges of an evolving health care system. *Psychology in the School, 45*(1), 74–87. https://doi.org/10.1002/pits.22154.

Sussman, R., & Gifford, R. (2019). Causality in the theory of planned behavior. *Personality and Social Psychology Bulletin, 45*(6), 920–33. https://doi.org/10.1177/0146167218801363.

Taras, H., & Potts-Datema, W. (2005). Obesity and student performance at school. *Journal of School Health 75*(8), 291–95. doi: 10.1111/j.1746-1561.2005.00040.x. PMID: 16179079.

Telljohann, S. K., Drake, J. A., & Price, J. H. (2004). Effect of full-time versus part-time school nurses on attendance of elementary students with asthma. *The Journal of School Nursing, 20*(6), 331–34. https://doi.org/10.1177%2F10598405040200060701.

Vestal, C. (2021, October 26). School nurse deficit deepens as states seek relief. The PEW Charitable Trust. https://www.pewtrusts.org/en/research-and-analysis/blogs/stateline/2021/10/26/school-nurse-deficit-deepens-as-states-seek-relief.

Wikel, K., & Markelz, A. M. (2023). School reentry program characteristics for students with chronic illness: A literature review. Manuscript accepted for publication. *Research, Advocacy, and Practice for Complex and Chronic Conditions, 41*(1).

Willgerodt, M. A., Brock, D. M., & Maughan, E. M. (2018). Public school nursing practice in the United States. *The Journal of School Nursing, 34*(3), 232–44. https://doi.org/10.1177%2F1059840517752456.

Zahran, H. S., Bailey, C. M., Damon, S. A., Garbe, P. L., & Breysse, P. N. (2018). Vital signs: Asthma in children—United States, 2001–2016. *MMWR. Morbidity and Mortality Weekly Report, 67*(5), 149–55. https://doi.org/10.15585/mmwr.mm6705e1.

Chapter 7

School Nurses

Partners in Educating Students with Health Concerns and Special Needs

Andrea Tanner and Cindy Hill

The best educators are always looking for ways to improve their students' academic outcomes and chances for success in the future. What if an evidence-based indicator of student success was just down the hallway? School nurse involvement in schools has been linked to improved student attendance and graduation rates, increased seat time where learning occurs, and rapid identification and response to communicable illnesses before they spread to teachers, staff, and students. This chapter will provide you with information that can help you partner with the school nurse to realize these positive outcomes for your students.

THE HISTORY OF SCHOOL NURSING

The specialty of school nursing was born out of a school-based experiment in New York City in 1902. Prior to the birth of this specialty, New York City hired 150 physicians to perform daily inspections of students to ensure contagious conditions such as impetigo and tuberculosis would not spread throughout the schools. Those students who appeared ill were sent home with a note many parents could not read or directions for a medication most parents could not afford. Students came home from school with the belief that a day out of school meant play time with friends outside of school, leading to more spread of illness among children rather than less. Nurses at the Henry Street Settlement were aware of social determinants of health long before the phrase became popular in health care and education. These nurses recommended a nurse work in tandem with physicians, providing direct care for students who could safely remain at school and conducting home visits for those who would benefit from family education on the condition and necessary treatment. Lina Rogers served as the first nurse in this role. Within six months of instituting school nursing services, absenteeism dropped by 90 percent.

THE NURSING PROCESS AND IMPLICATIONS FOR EDUCATORS

To achieve such remarkable results as Lina Rogers and the Henry Street Settlement nurses, school nurses use a process familiar to any middle school science student—the scientific process. However, the five-step process has been fine tuned for the unique skillset of school nurses.

First, school nurses perform an assessment. This assessment can be for an individual student who enters the health office with a complaint of illness or injury, a group of students who became ill with similar symptoms within the same classroom, or an entire school in need of improved physical activity and nutrition lifestyle choices. In every instance listed, the teacher's observations can be a valuable piece in the puzzle of student health. Teachers are often the first to hear a health complaint, witness an accident that results in injury, or observe a schoolwide concern that could benefit from a school nurse's intervention. While teachers and school nurses cannot diagnose medical conditions, they can collaborate to collect key information that can help in the second step of the nursing process.

The second step in the nursing process is developing a nursing diagnosis. For instance, a school nurse cannot diagnose a student with type 1 diabetes, but the school nurse can identify signs of symptoms of this medical condition, such as frequent urination, rapid weight loss, and extreme thirst, and recommend to the family that they should seek medical care. In the case of a student with newly diagnosed type 1 diabetes, the school nurse may identify several appropriate nursing diagnoses, such as (in layperson terms) risk for unstable blood sugar levels, need for an effective medication and treatment regimen, and readiness for the student to cope with the new diagnosis.

The third step is identifying outcomes and planning to reach those outcomes. Much like developing an individualized education program (IEP) with targeted goals, school nurses address each nursing diagnosis with relevant outcomes and a strategy to reach those outcomes. For a student with type 1 diabetes, a plan might include the school nurse monitoring blood sugar prior to a student leaving school on a bus, training many school personnel on the use of emergency injectable or nasal medication, tediously following medical orders for insulin administration, and arranging a support group meeting to introduce the student to peers who have been managing type 1 diabetes. Desired outcomes could include blood sugar readings within normal limits and evidence of effective coping at least 75 percent of the time. Teachers and other school personnel may play a role in identifying a student's health care learning needs or planning for a medical emergency response in class, on a field trip, or during a school crisis event.

The fourth step is implementing the nursing care plan. School nurses have numerous interventions they may apply to meet the specific needs of every student, ranging from motivational interviewing and self-management education for improved self-care of chronic diseases to care coordination to address poorly managed conditions. For students with type 1 diabetes, the school nurse may conduct annual trainings to ensure staff are prepared to identify and respond to life-threatening low blood sugars quickly, provide self-management training that helps the student rely less and less on others for diabetes care decisions, and refer the student and family to a mental health care provider if signs of depression related to the diagnosis are detected.

Finally, the fifth step in the nursing process is evaluation. This includes monitoring the student's health status and effectiveness of implemented nursing care as a continuous feedback loop. This feedback involves notification to parent/guardian for referrals when needed. Teachers' insight into how the school nurse plan is affecting the student's ability to feel healthy, focus on learning, and be inside the classroom learning (rather than in the health office) is extremely valuable in the evaluation process. Textbox 7.1 depicts a sample individualized care plan for a student with type 1 diabetes. School nurses can develop an individualized care plan for any health condition that requires school nurse and school personnel involvement for daily routine care, prevention of emergencies, and recognition and response to medical emergencies.

TEXTBOX 7.1.
Individualized Health Care Plan (IHP)

Student: _____

School: _____

Grade: _____ School Year: _____

IHP Completed by: _____ Date: _____

IHP Review Dates: _____

Nursing Assessment Review Dates: _____

Nursing Assessment Completed by: _____ Date: _____

Nursing Diagnosis	Sample Interventions and Activities	Date Implemented	Sample Outcome Indicator	Date Evaluated
Managing Potential Diabetes Emergencies (risk for unstable blood glucose)	Establish and document student's routine for maintaining blood glucose within goal range including while at school: • Where to check blood glucose: ☐ Classroom ☐ Health room ☐ Other: _____ • When to check blood glucose: ☐ Before breakfast ☐ Mid-morning ☐ Before lunch ☐ After lunch ☐ Before snack ☐ Before PE ☐ After PE ☐ Two hours after correction dose ☐ Before dismissal ☐ As needed ☐ Other: _____ • Student's self-care skills: ☐ Independent ☐ Supervision ☐ Full assistance • Brand/model of BG meter: _____ • Brand/model of CGM: _____		**Blood glucose remains in goal range** Percentage of time 0% 25% 50% 75% 100%	

Nursing Diagnosis	Sample Interventions and Activities	Date Implemented	Sample Outcome Indicator	Date Evaluated
Supporting the Independent Student (effective therapeutic regimen management)	**Hypoglycemia Management** **STUDENT WILL:** • Check blood glucose when hypoglycemia suspected • Treat hypoglycemia (follow Emergency Care Plans for Hypoglycemia and Hyperglycemia) • Take action following a hypoglycemia episode • Keep quick-acting glucose product to treat on the spot • Type: _____ • Routinely monitor hypoglycemia trends r/t class schedule (for example, time of PE, scheduled lunch, recess) and insulin dosing • Report to and consult with parents/guardians, school nurse, HCP, and school personnel as appropriate		**Monitors blood glucose and appropriately responds to results** Percentage of time 0% 25% 50% 75% 100%	
Supporting Positive Coping Skills (readiness for enhanced coping)	**Create Positive School Environment** • Ensure confidentiality • Discuss with parents/guardians and student preferences about how the school can support student's coping skills • Collaborate with parents/guardians and school personnel to meet student's coping needs • Collaborate with school personnel to create an accepting and understanding environment		**Demonstrates positive coping** Percentage of time 0% 25% 50% 75% 100%	

Note: From National Institutes of Health (https://www.niddk.nih.gov/-/media/Files/Health-Information/Health-Professionals/Diabetes/health-care-professionals/Individualized_Healthcare_Plan.docx).

FRAMEWORK FOR TWENTY-FIRST-CENTURY SCHOOL NURSING PRACTICE

While modern day school clinics may look vastly different than that of the Henry Street Settlement in New York, current school nursing practice maintains the same focus on exacting standards of quality health care and critical outcomes related to health and academics. The National Association of School Nurses (NASN) has developed the *Framework for 21st Century School Nursing Practice*™ to depict the multifaceted role of school nurses. See figure 7.1 for a full depiction and explanation of the school nursing framework.

As depicted in the framework, school nurses are guided by standards of practice as well as their state practice act through which they are licensed, much like a teacher works under a teaching license within their state. The model for school nursing practice revolves around student-centered care. The main goal for school nurses is to keep students safe and healthy so they can continue learning and growing. This care is also family centered to include the needs of families with whom the student lives and interacts. The framework also highlights four key principles: care coordination, quality improvement, community/public health, and leadership. These principles guide the nurse to provide optimal care for students and staff in their school setting.

Care coordination is often the most recognizable aspect of school nursing. All care given by a school nurse is either within the independent scope of nursing practice or in accordance with a prescriber's (physician, advanced practice nurse, or physician's assistant) current order for care. A prescriber may order a medication to be administered or a medical procedure to be done so a student can remain in school learning. These prescribed tasks and other relevant nursing activities are coordinated by the school nurse and documented in nursing care plans. Such plans may also include the education of teachers and staff regarding a student's health needs and the delegation of certain tasks when the school nurse is unavailable.

As a part of the continuous feedback loop of the nursing process, school nurses ensure quality improvement within their practice. Quality improvement requires school nurses to maintain records of the care they provide and screenings they perform, measure outcomes that result from their care, and contribute data to state and/or national unified data collection efforts. The data school nurses create and collect through their care coordination efforts are critical to informing local, state, and national child health policy, advocacy, and practice initiatives.

Another critical role of the school nurse is to monitor and provide nursing care for students exhibiting signs or symptoms of illnesses and impairments in the school setting. This monitoring of student health allows the nurse to better comprehend the surrounding community's health needs. Nurses will often assess and monitor for annual flu outbreaks and other contagious

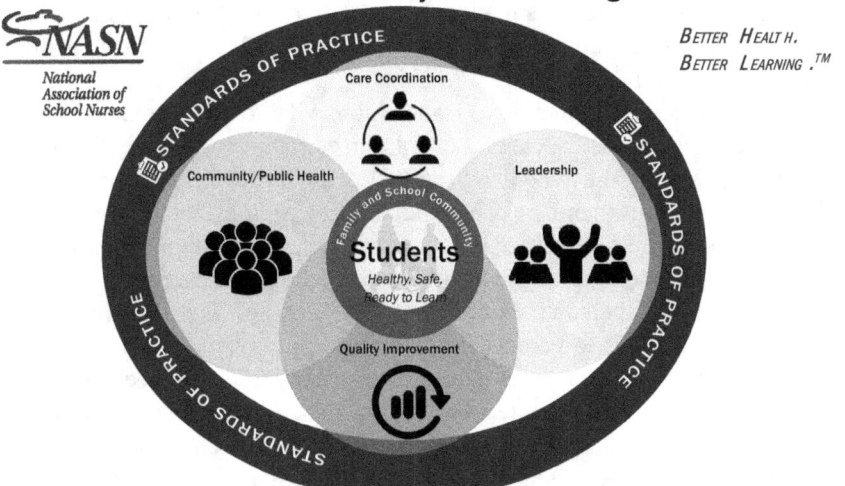

NASN's *Framework for 21st Century School Nursing Practice*™ (the *Framework*) provides structure and focus for the key principles and components of current day, evidence-based school nursing practice. It is aligned with the Whole School, Whole Community, Whole Child model that calls for a collaborative approach to learning and health (ASCD & CDC, 2014). Central to the *Framework* is student-centered nursing care that occurs within the context of the students' family and school community. Surrounding the students, family, and school community are the non-hierarchical, overlapping key principles of *Care Coordination, Leadership, Quality Improvement,* and *Community/Public Health*. These principles are surrounded by the fifth principle, *Standards of Practice*, which is foundational for evidence-based, clinically competent, quality care. School nurses daily use the skills outlined in the practice components of each principle to help students be healthy, safe, and ready to learn.

ASCD & CDC. (2014). *Whole school whole community whole child: A collaborative approach to learning and health.* Retrieved from http://www.ascd.org/ASCD/pdf/siteASCD/publications/wholechild/wscc-a-collaborative-approach.pdf

© National Association of School Nurses, 2015   Rev. 10/6/16

Figure 7.1.   Framework for 21st Century School Nursing Practice™
Source: National Association of School Nurses, 2015. Copyright © 2015 by National Association of School Nurses. Reprinted with permission. https://higherlogicdownload.s3.amazonaws.com/NASN/8575d1b7-94ad-45ab-808e-d45019cc5c08/UploadedImages/PDFs/Framework%20for%2021st%20Century%20School%20Nursing%20Practice/21stCenturySchoolNurseFramework2016onepager.pdf.

infections such as measles and E. coli. Additionally, school nurses assess students for vision and hearing deficits through routine early detection screenings. Certain state laws mandate annual screenings in the school setting to assess current population health needs, especially when those health needs might interfere with optimal learning.

The final framework principle of leadership is vital to school nurses influencing student health and success. School nurses routinely work as the lone health care provider in a school setting that often has over 750 students as well as over 100 staff members. They may also be responsible for the health and well-being of multiple school buildings and delegation of nursing tasks to many nonnurse personnel. Daily, the nurse may assess and care for over 100 students or staff members in their health offices or clinics. This does not even include the phone calls to parents and health care providers, documentation of care and communication, tracking illnesses reported on absentee lists, and attending Section 504 and IEP team meetings. School nurses may also oversee school or district health and wellness initiatives and committees, serve as preceptors for nursing students, lead within nursing and school nursing organizations, and advocate for school health change at the local, state, and national political levels. Learning to lead in school health is what allows the nurse to run the health clinic efficiently, promote health outside the clinic, and provide the best care for positive health outcomes for students.

This leadership does not always come naturally but can be learned in the nurse's college education. There are various levels of education and licensure for entry into their nursing career. For registered nurses (RNs), they may take a national competency exam called the NCLEX after completing a two- to three-year associate degree or a four-year bachelor's degree. For a school nurse, a minimum of a bachelor's degree ensures appropriate coursework in leadership, pediatric nursing, and community/public health nursing. This coursework will equip RNs as they work independently within their scope of practice in the school setting. Nurses can demonstrate proficiency by becoming certified in their nursing specialty. School nurses can become certified in school nursing (Nationally Certified School Nurse, or NCSN), pediatrics (Certified Pediatric Nurse, or CPN), or public health (Certified in Public Health, or CPH). Finally, in some states, nurses can obtain state certification in school nursing through their state department of education or department of health.

LAWS REGARDING EDUCATING STUDENTS WITH HEALTH CARE NEEDS

As health care professionals practicing in an education setting, school nurses must be familiar with and abide by laws pertaining to education, nursing, and general health care. The following sections provide a brief overview of each category and how school nurses and teachers must collaborate to ensure legal compliance.

Education Laws

Various laws have been enacted in the United States to protect students with special health care needs from discrimination and provides for their needs for an appropriate education. Section 504 of the Rehabilitation Act of 1973 prohibits discrimination against students with disabilities. The Americans with Disabilities Act Amendments Act of 2008 affected the meaning of the term disability within Section 504. The Individuals with Disabilities Act (IDEA) of 1975 is a grant statute that funds special education programs, with many specific rules and regulations for schools who receive federal IDEA funding (US Department of Education Office for Civil Rights, 2020).

Section 504 and IDEA provide differing definitions of disability; however, students who qualify as having a disability under either law are entitled to the provision of a free appropriate public education. Qualifying for services or accommodations under Section 504 requires having an impairment that substantially limits a major life activity; qualifying under IDEA for an IEP requires being between the ages of three and twenty-one years and meeting the criteria of one of thirteen disability categories as well as having a special educational need. The purpose of IDEA is to provide needed services to children with a qualifying disability to enhance their education and promote student success. This federal law also provides early intervention services to qualifying infants up to two years of age. Even if denied services under IDEA, a parent/guardian can request accommodations under Section 504. Whether a student receives services under IDEA, Section 504, or a school nurse–developed individualized health plan, it is vital that the school teacher include the school nurse in the sharing of any updated health information and meetings that involve the student's plan of care. Together, teachers and nurses can collaborate to ensure positive health and academic outcomes for students.

In addition to laws that protect students with disabilities from discrimination and ensure appropriate services and accommodations are provided, another law protects the privacy of students' health and academic information provided to or generated by the school. The federally enacted Family Educational Rights and Privacy Act (FERPA) of 1974 protects students' educational information (educational, health, and personal information) from misuse. While student information is protected, provisions are made within the law to allow the sharing of health information with school personnel with "legitimate education interests." Information can also be shared with health care providers and other entities with prior written consent from a parent or guardian (US Department of Education, 2021).

Nursing Laws

Upon passing the national licensure exam called NCLEX, nurses work under their state licensure laws and regulations. It is important to note that often the guidelines in the school setting for nurses are different than for other professions such as teachers. Nurses work under their state practice act that provides guidelines for ethical, safe care and the delegation of that care to nonnurses.

During important student planning meetings such as IEP and Section 504 team meetings, all staff involved in student care will develop a plan of care to be implemented for the school year. If your school employs a registered nurse, by state law, this nurse will have a broader scope of practice than a licensed practical nurse.

Health Care Laws

The main health care law applicable in the school setting is the Health Insurance Portability and Accountability Act (HIPAA) Privacy Rule, especially if the school employs health care providers who bill Medicaid for services provided according to a student's IEP. This federal law enacted in 1996 protects sensitive, confidential data from being transmitted or shared with others without the written permission of the patient or guardian. Many schools may be considered HIPAA-covered entities if school nurses provide health care services during the schools' normal course of business. However, most schools do not have to comply with the HIPAA Privacy Rule requirements because the only health records maintained or shared are "education records" covered under FERPA, which are excluded from the definition of "protected health information" (Department of Education, 2019). Certain student health information can be shared in the right context such as students' IEP or 504 plans, emergency action plans shared with substitute teachers and bus drivers, or in the event of public emergencies such as illness outbreaks.

THE IMPACT OF SCHOOL NURSES ON THE EDUCATION SETTING

With respect to the role of school nurses in modern day schools, much has remained the same since the days of Lina Rogers in New York City. School nurses are still credited with the rapid identification and response to communicable diseases, as evidenced by a New York school nurse lauded for her role in identifying the first swine flu cluster in 2009 (Hartocollis, 2009). School nurses also play an increasingly vital role in ensuring students are in the classroom learning as much as possible. While many schools employ nonnurse personnel, or health aides, to care for and make decisions about whether students go home or return to class, school nurses send far fewer students home from school than nonnurse counterparts (Pennington & Delaney, 2008). This allows more students to be in class learning, decreasing the chances of a health condition, illness, or injury affecting students' access to education. The presence of school nurses in schools is also credited with improved overall student attendance (Yoder, 2020), decreased chronic absenteeism (Jacobsen, Meeder, & Voskuil, 2016), and increased student seat time (Rau & Lytle, 2020). With increased opportunities to learn, it is no surprise that school nurses may also impact graduation rates and standardized test scores (Darnell, Hager, & Loprinzi, 2019).

Although school nurses' focus on student-centered outcomes is of highest priority based upon the framework, school nurses make crucial differences in the lives of not only students but also the entire school team. For instance, school nurses save principals almost one hour, teachers twenty minutes, and clerical staff forty-five minutes per day (Baisch, Lundeen, & Murphy, 2011). This time savings also equates to financial savings when those hours and minutes are tabulated per hourly wage (over $130,000 per year in 2011, which was well over the cost of employing a school nurse). In addition to school-specific personnel time and money savings, school nurses drove societal financial savings of $2.20 for every $1 spent on school nursing through prevented medical care costs, parental productivity loss, and teacher productivity loss (Wang et al., 2014).

SCHOOL NURSE ROLE IN EDUCATING STUDENTS WITH HEALTH CONCERNS

Care of students with various diagnoses and health concerns is varied and detailed to address problems identified during the nursing assessment as well as specific written orders from the student's provider, when needed by law.

Allergies

Roughly two students in every classroom have a food allergy (National Center for Chronic Disease Prevention and Health Promotion, 2022). There are many other allergens students may react negatively to, including insect stings and latex. This means every school employee needs to know their role in recognizing the signs of a potentially life-threatening allergic reaction, called anaphylaxis, and knowing how to respond if one occurs. Signs of anaphylaxis are the same, no matter the cause of the reaction. That means stings may cause much more than just skin swelling and food may cause much more than throat swelling or vomiting. The most common signs of anaphylaxis that you can recognize without any special knowledge or equipment include

- skin (hives, itching, redness, or severe paleness),
- throat and airway (swollen tongue or throat, difficulty or high-pitched noises while breathing, cough or hoarseness),
- digestive issues (nausea, vomiting, diarrhea, or cramping), and
- blood flow through body (complaints of dizziness/light-headedness, feelings of confusion/anxiety or impending doom).

Students with known allergy concerns should have an emergency action plan and emergency medication (an epinephrine autoinjector) readily available at school. Many times, all school employees are taught how to use this lifesaving medication. If you work closely with a student with a known allergy, stay in close contact with the school nurse and receive updated training as needed to be prepared.

Asthma

At least one in every twelve school-aged children has asthma (Centers for Disease Control and Prevention, 2018). Asthma is a leading cause of illness-related school absences (Hsu et al., 2016). Teachers should understand the basic physical complications students experience with asthma. First, the airways, or system of tubes that make up the lungs, swell and become narrow. Imagine normal breathing feeling like breathing through a restaurant straw; then imagine breathing through a coffee stirrer instead. Second, the airways may become filled with mucus, making it even harder to breathe. During asthma "attacks," the muscles that surround the airways can become even more narrowed as muscles that wrap around the airways tighten. Asthma is not feeling "winded" after running and playing; it is a chronic condition that can be life threatening.

Educators can play a significant role in assisting students with asthma, including

- understanding triggers that can cause asthma attacks (allergens, chemicals like cleaning products and air fresheners, pet dander, smoke, cold air, exercise, or having a cold),

- recognizing symptoms of asthma "attacks" or "flareups" (chest feeling tight, coughing, feeling short of breath, whistling sound when breathing out especially), and
- knowing how to respond when asthma symptoms occur at school (such as contacting the school nurse if one is present, following an individualized health care plan for inhaler or nebulizer use, or calling 911 if symptoms become severe to the point of extreme difficulty breathing that makes it hard to walk or talk, lips or fingers turning blue, or feeling like passing out).

Autism Spectrum Disorder

Autism Spectrum Disorder (ASD) is a diagnosis of a broad range of disorders that usually encompasses the child having notable deficits in both social and communication skills (Oriel et al., 2020). This makes learning in the school environment challenging for the child with an autism diagnosis. Often, this diagnosis for the child will not happen until the child is in a school environment. Teachers noticing the child not achieving grade-level goals can communicate with the parent as well as the school nurse for assessment. Included in the diagnosis assessment will be a vision and often a hearing assessment for the child. Referrals can be made to a medical provider for a diagnosis. Depending on the plan of care, the student may take daily medications that will be administered in the nurse's clinic as well as attend speech and occupational therapies. See figure 7.2 for the various categories and dimensions for diagnosing ASD and overlap with other conditions and symptoms.

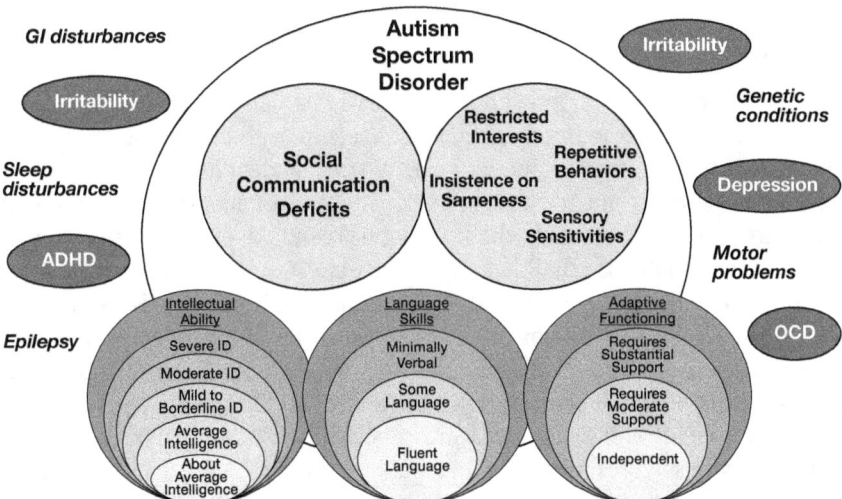

Figure 7.2. Overlap between Categories and Dimensions for Autism Spectrum Disorder and Other Conditions

Source: Rosen, Lord, & Volkmar, 2021. CC BY 4.0, http://creativecommons.org/licenses/by/4.0.

Diabetes

Diabetes is the third most common chronic health issue in children under age twenty, with 98 percent of diabetes cases in school-aged children falling under the category of type 1 diabetes (Pettitt et al., 2014). In the school setting, the nurse works closely with the student with type 1 diabetes, parents, and teachers to ensure that the student can safely stay in school learning. Following a very specific medical plan from the health care provider, the school nurse will assist the student with blood sugar (glucose) checks, calculating carbohydrates eaten in meals and snacks, considering activity levels throughout the day, and determining appropriate insulin doses given multiple times during the school day. Students with diabetes will visit the clinic often for assistance to

- drop off/pick up supplies,
- check blood sugar,
- administer insulin,
- eat a snack to ensure enough sugar is in the body for exercise in PE/recess, and
- check devices such as glucose monitor and/or insulin pump.

These visits will happen daily, usually multiple times per day, and the nurse will communicate often with the student's teacher for planning of care in the school setting. Consistent care of blood sugar keeps the student in the classroom learning and increases the likelihood of a healthier future.

Seizures

In a school of one thousand students, at least six students are likely to have epilepsy, a seizure disorder that results in students with the condition missing eleven or more days of school per year. When a student has a known seizure condition, seizures are not an emergency in and of themselves. However, there are steps teachers and school personnel can take to ensure any seizure triggers are avoided if possible and students are safe in the event of seizures (Centers for Disease Control and Prevention, 2022). Many seizure triggers cannot be avoided at school but are helpful to be aware of, such as sleep deprivation, poor diet, caffeine consumption, menstrual cycle/hormonal changes, missed medication, and illness (Schachter, 2022). Seizures can also be triggered by flashing lights and stress, both of which can happen at school. Students with seizures may have an aura, or warning, before a severe seizure occurs. Auras can include changes in sensations, such as visual disturbances, odd sensations of smell or taste, tingling or numbness, or sense of déjà vu.

Students can experience myriad types of seizures. Some are easier to recognize than others. Seizures may look like staring into space, uncontrollable movement of one or both sides of the body while remaining responsive, or complete unresponsiveness with uncontrollable body movements.

Some students with seizures do not have epilepsy. Seizures can occur from a recent head injury, low blood sugar, or from a mental health condition called functional neurological disorder (also known as psychogenic nonepileptic seizures). The primary goal for seizure response for any cause remains safety.

For students with a known seizure condition from an epileptic or nonepileptic cause, work with the school nurse to better understand the specific details and response plan for each student with seizures. Some students with epileptic seizures may also have an emergency plan for seizure rescue medication, which might be given in the nose, mouth, rectum, or injected into the skin.

Mental Health Conditions

Nursing involves assessing and caring for the whole child in the school setting. One component often seen in the busy school day is the assessment of mental health needs of children. Many factors such as past trauma, biological, and social factors can impact a child's state of mental health. As a child ages, conditions such as depression and anxiety as well as behavior disorders can show symptoms such as distress and intense fear while in the school setting (Perron et al., 2021). Children might exhibit stress and anxiety over

- new environments,
- learning new concepts,
- being away from family/guardians,
- test taking, and
- normal body changes in adolescence.

Working closely alongside the nurse, the teacher can assist with identifying potential root causes of worsened mental health symptoms and work interprofessionally toward the improvement of the child's mental health symptoms and school experience.

Medical Device and Procedure Needs

Technology advances have brought more mobility to students with special health care needs. Students attend school with various medical devices to aid in their daily activities or a need for medical procedures while in the school setting. While these devices or procedures can seem complicated, the nurse works closely with the student and teachers to ensure the student can safely remain in school learning. The school nurse develops an individualized health care plan including tasks required to keep the student healthy and safe, who is responsible for each task, and how to respond to any device or procedure emergencies. School personnel may encounter the following medical devices and procedures:

- Ostomy: a rerouting of how stool exits the body. A stoma, or opening, is formed on the abdomen and covered by a pouch to collect stool. Care during the school day may include emptying or changing the pouch.
- G-tube: a device placed in the abdomen to allow direct access to the stomach for feeding, hydration, and administering medications. While at school, school personnel should be aware of how to respond if the g-tube is accidentally removed or leaks fluids. If accidentally removed, the g-tube must be replaced quickly to prevent the hole from closing. Depending on state laws and school policies and procedures, some school personnel may be trained to administer prescribed food, drink, or medications.
- Urinary catheter: a tube placed into the bladder to empty the body of urine. Catheters may be indwelling (always stay in the body and collect urine into a bag) or inserted intermittently to remove urine at scheduled times during the day. If a student who is unable to remove urine through elimination is not catheterized for an extended period, many complications can incur, including pain and bladder, kidney, or bloodstream infections.
- Tracheostomy tube: a device placed into an opening made in the neck that rests inside the windpipe (trachea). The device allows air to enter the lungs through the tube in the neck rather than the nose or mouth. The accidental removal of the tube is life threatening; many schools ensure a nurse or other trained professional is with or near the student with a tracheostomy tube any time the student is at school or a school-related activity.
- Wheelchair: Students who are unable to stand or walk safely may require a wheelchair to transport them from place to place within and around the school. Wheelchairs may require being manually pushed by the student or others or may be motorized by a battery. Depending on each student's needs, time out of the wheelchair may be scheduled during the school day. Students can get pressure sores if they are not repositioned throughout the day. Students who require wheelchairs for mobilization in school should have an evacuation plan for how to safely exit the building in an emergency and who will assist.
- Mobility devices: In addition to wheelchairs to assist mobility, students may use orthotic braces to support their legs or crutches, canes, or walk-

ers to assist with weakness or unsteadiness. These devices should be prescribed by a health care provider and require training for students to ensure they are used properly.

Transition Readiness to Adult Care

School personnel work diligently to assist the student with special health care needs to achieve academic goals and graduate from high school. Around the time of graduation, another transition occurs—the health care transition from pediatric to adult care. For youth with special health care needs, this transition is often missed. Yearly in the United States, 750,000 youth with special health care needs reach the age of eighteen, yet only 17 percent achieve the transition goals of becoming independent (Lebrun-Harris et al., 2018). These transition goals are tasks that school personnel (teachers, nurses, and other therapy staff) can assist the student in reaching. These goals are set and included in the student's yearly IEP plan and should detail the specific student goals needed to gain independence in activities of daily living and managing specific health care needs. While this will look different for every child, the overarching goal is for school personnel to assist with student transition readiness throughout the school experience.

HOW TO PARTNER WITH SCHOOL NURSES FOR STUDENT HEALTH AND SUCCESS

Students are most successful when they are surrounded by an interdisciplinary team of professionals dedicated to student success and overall well-being. However, the interdisciplinary team of educators and support personnel cannot make an impact on student success and well-being unless they effectively collaborate with one another. Here are a few tips for ensuring you are collaborating with school nurses to appreciate what they can do to improve students' academic and health outcomes:

- Routinely discuss student health concern observations to the school nurse to inform assessment and evaluation processes.
  Share any health-related updates from parents with the school nurse.
- Collaborate to ensure students with the greatest health care needs are prioritized, which may mean being judicious about what students are sent to the school nurse for nonemergent situations (a days-old bruise with no concern for abuse or a bleeding scab from an injury that occurred over the weekend).

- Know what must be communicated and to whom (including concerns about possible student abuse or neglect, bullying, lack of necessary medical care, possible seizures, injuries incurred from faulty school equipment, patterns of illness or injury that may require nursing intervention, or obvious medication side effects).
- Know what should not be communicated (including opinions about medication or condition treatment options—it is best to leave these conversations to the school nurse).
- Include the school nurse on formal meetings for student care including IEP or 504 meetings for initial or annual review.

REFERENCES

Baisch, M. J., Lundeen, S. P., & Murphy, M. K. (2011). Evidence-based research on the value of school nurses in an urban school system. *Journal of School Health, 81*(2), 74–80. https://doi.org/10.1111/j.1746-1561.2010.00563.x.

Centers for Disease Control and Prevention (2018). Vital signs: Asthma in children. https://www.cdc.gov/vitalsigns/pdf/2018-02-vitalsigns.pdf.

Centers for Disease Control and Prevention (2022, February). Epilepsy. CDC Healthy Schools. https://www.cdc.gov/healthyschools/npao/epilepsy.htm.

Darnell, T., Hager, K., & Loprinzi, P. D. (2019). The impact of school nurses in Kentucky public high schools. *Journal of School Nursing, 35*(6), 434–41. https://doi.org/10.1177/1059840518785954.

Department of Education. (2019). Joint guidance on the application of the Family Educational Rights and Privacy Act (FERPA) and the Health Insurance Portability and Accountability Act of 1996 (HIPAA) to Student Health Records.

Epilepsy Foundation (2020). *Seizure first aid: How to help someone having a seizure* [Graphic]. https://www.epilepsy.com/sites/default/files/atoms/files/SFA%20Flier_HQ_8.5x11_PDF.pdf.

Hartocollis, A. (2009, April 28). School nurse's response to flu wins applause. *New York Times*. https://www.nytimes.com/2009/04/29/nyregion/29nurse.html.

Hsu, J., Qin, X., Beavers, S. F., & Mirabelli, M. C. (2016). Asthma-related school absenteeism, morbidity, and modifiable factors. *American Journal of Preventive Medicine, 51*(1), 23–32. https://doi.org/10.1016/j.amepre.2015.12.012.

Jacobsen, K., Meeder, L., & Voskuil, V. R. (2016). Chronic student absenteeism: The critical role of school nurses. *NASN School Nurse (Print), 31*(3), 178–85. https://doi.org/10.1177/1942602X16638855.

Lebrun-Harris, L. A., McManus, M. A., Ilango, S. M., Cyr, M., McLellan, S. B., Mann, M. Y., & White, P. H. (2018). Transition planning among US youth with and without special health care needs. *Pediatrics, 142*(4), 1–11. http://publications.aap.org/pediatrics/article-pdf/142/4/e20180194/1065762/peds_20180194.pdf.

National Association of School Nurses (2015). *Framework for 21st century school nursing practice*[TM]. https://higherlogicdownload.s3.amazonaws.com

/NASN/8575d1b7-94ad-45ab-808e-d45019cc5c08/UploadedImages/PDFs/Framework%20for%202lst%20Century%20School%20Nursing%20Practice/21stCentury SchoolNurseFramework2016onepager.pdf.

National Center for Chronic Disease Prevention and Health Promotion. (2022, February 24). Food allergies. CDC Health Schools. https://www.cdc.gov/healthyschools/foodallergies/index.htm.

Oriel, K. N., Reed, T., Saufley, R., Wetzel, E., & Wilt, C. (2020). Utilization of physical activity in school-based settings for children with autism spectrum disorder. *Palaestra, 34*(4), 44–49.

Pennington, N., & Delaney, E. (2008). The number of students sent home by school nurses compared to unlicensed personnel. *Journal of School Nursing, 24*(5), 290–97. https://doi.org/10.1177/1059840508322382.

Perron, T., Jakubowski, T., Razzi, C., & Kartoz, C. (2021). Mental health assessment of the frequent visitors in the school setting-Part 1: An overview. *NASN School Nurse, 36*(4), 197–204. https://doi.org/10.1177/1942602X21996442.

Pettitt, D. J., Talton, J., Dabelea, D., Divers, J., Imperatore, G., Lawrence, J. M., Liese, A. D., Linder, B., Mayer-Davis, E. J., Pihoker, C., Saydah, S. H., Standiford, D. A., & Hamman, R. F. (2014). Prevalence of diabetes in U.S. youth in 2009: The SEARCH for diabetes in youth study. *Diabetes Care, 37*(2), 402–8. https://doi.org/10.2337/dc13-1838.

Rau, W., & Lytle, M. (2020). The role of the school nurse in increasing instructional time using multi-tiered systems of support for behavior (MTSS-B): A quality improvement project. *NASN School Nurse (Print), 35*(5), 276–83. https://doi.org/10.1177/1942602X20942492

Rosen, N. E., Lord, C., and Volkmar, F. R. (2021). The diagnosis of autism: From Kanner to DSM-III to DSM-5 and beyond. *Journal of Autism and Developmental Disorders, 51*, 4253–70. https://doi.org/10.1007/s10803-021-04904-1.

Schachter, S. (2022). Seizure triggers. Epilepsy Foundation. https://www.epilepsy.com/what-is-epilepsy/seizure-triggers.

US Department of Education. (2021, August 25). Family Educational Rights and Privacy Act (FERPA). https://www2.ed.gov/policy/gen/guid/fpco/ferpa/index.html.

US Department of Education Office for Civil Rights (2020). Protecting students with disabilities: Frequently asked questions about Section 504 and the education of children with disabilities. https://www2.ed.gov/about/offices/list/ocr/504faq.html.

Wang, L. Y., Vernon-Smiley, M., Gapinski, M. A., Desisto, M., Maughan, E., & Sheetz, A. (2014). Cost-benefit study of school nursing services. *JAMA Pediatrics, 168*(7), 642–48. https://doi.org/10.1001/jamapediatrics.2013.5441.

Yoder, C. M. K. (2020). School nurses and student academic outcomes: An integrative review. *Journal of School Nursing, 36*(1), 49–60. https://doi.org/10.1177/1059840518824397.

Chapter 8

Recovery High Schools
Working at the Intersection of Education, Mental Health, and Addiction Science

Linda Gagyi and Rachelle Gardner

Recovery high schools are secondary schools designed specifically to meet the needs of students in recovery from substance use disorders or cooccurring disorders (Association of Recovery Schools, www.recoveryschools.org). Recovery high schools serve a unique population of students, with the goal of meeting their mental health and recovery needs as well as their educational needs. The primary goal of recovery high schools is to support students in recovery from substance use disorders while providing them with the resources to meet state requirements for a secondary school diploma. The staff of recovery high schools are drawn from the fields of education and mental health, with the staff often including administrative staff, special education and general education teachers, substance misuse counselors, and mental health professionals. Working as a team, these professionals provide students in recovery from substance use disorders with both a high school education and supports for their recovery.

In this chapter we will present evidence of the prevalence of substance use disorders in the adolescent population of the United States, as well as the need for recovery high schools and the unique role they play in the continuum of care. We will then focus on one recovery high school, Hope Academy, and describe the professional collaboration between the educational and mental health staff in the service of their students.

PREVALENCE OF SUBSTANCE USE DISORDERS IN THE UNITED STATES

Substance use disorders in the United States affected more than 1.6 million young people between the ages of twelve and seventeen in 2020; however, little more than 120,000 of these young people received treatment (Substance Abuse and Mental Health Services Administration, 2021). For young people in recovery the school environment is often the single greatest hazard to their success in maintaining sobriety (Botzet et al., 2014), which is illustrated by the fact that nearly 80 percent of all young people in recovery return to drug use within a year after returning to traditional high school (Fairbanks, 2016; Winters et al., 2000).

Substance use disorders occur when recurrent use of alcohol and/or drugs causes "clinically significant impairment, including health problems, disability, and failure to meet major responsibilities at work, school, or home" (Substance Abuse and Mental Health Services Administration, 2021). Substance use disorder prevalence rises sharply after age twelve and peaks between ages eighteen and twenty-three (Substance Abuse and Mental Health Services Administration, 2021; Young et al., 2002). National data shows that nearly half (47 percent) of young people in eighth through twelfth grade admitted use of any illicit drug in the past thirty days, and almost one-third (28.4 percent) consumed alcohol within the same timespan (Johnston et al., 2010). Despite the prevalence of substance abuse among adolescents, there has been a consistent gap between the number of students needing treatment and the amount of treatment available. In 2013, there were an approximate 120,000 young people in the United States aged twelve to seventeen in recovery treatment programs for substance use disorders, which still left more than 1.2 million individuals in need of treatment. Most of the young people who received substance use disorder treatment did so in outpatient facilities (87 percent), with the remainder split between nonhospital residential treatment and hospital inpatient treatment facilities (Substance Abuse and Mental Health Services Administration, CBHSQ Report, 2013).

A variety of biological and cultural factors make young people particularly vulnerable to substance use disorders. One important factor is that the prefrontal cortex, the area of the brain responsible for impulse control and decision making, remains underdeveloped until an individual reaches their mid-twenties. This area is also indicated in the pharmacological processes of substance use disorders (Chambers, Taylor, & Potenza, 2003). Additionally, young people are less inclined to seek help for drug use than their adult counterparts, and evidence suggests a young person's willingness to undergo treatment is proportional to the amount of negative consequences he or she has experienced in their relatively short lifespan (Breda & Heflinger, 2004). Moreover, young people, compared to adults, are more likely to conceal their substance use and maintain such behaviors even after occurrences with the criminal justice system (NIDA, 2014). Last, young people are prone to taking risks and rebelling against authority, which makes them especially susceptible to the negative effects of substance use (Jainchill, 2012).

Unfortunately, the effects of substance use disorders can often carry over into adulthood, considering the majority of adults with substance use disorders report their drug use began during adolescence (Cohen et al., 2007; Dennis et al., 2002). The negative effects of substance use disorders among young people include, but are not limited to, illness, poverty, reduced grades, family and social problems, school and work performance, legal and criminal justice issues, diminished memory and cognitive abilities, problems obtaining and maintaining employment, and a decreased probability of finishing high school or attending university (Brown & Tapert, 2004; Homel, Thompson, & Leadbeater, 2014; Larm et al., 2008; Lisdahl et al., 2014; Menasco & Blair, 2014; Newcomb & Bentler, 1988; Patrick, Schulenberg, & O'Malley, 2013; Squeglia, Jacobus, & Tapert, 2009; Thoma et al., 2011). However, young people who are identified and treated for substance use disorders early are capable of progressing into adulthood with minimal disruptions. Therefore, given the numerous negative effects, it's crucial that we understand programs that are effective in helping young people recover from substance use disorders.

THE ROLE OF THE HIGH SCHOOL IN SUBSTANCE USE DISORDERS

Nearly one in four high school students in the United States is provided with an illicit drug on school property (Kann et al., 2000) and nearly all young people in recovery who return to their original high school posttreatment report being offered drugs on their first day back (Vaillant, 1988). As a result, the school environment has a great deal of influence on the success or failure of a young person in recovery. Evidence suggests that academic achievement, interest in school, and association with nonusing peers can all be protective factors against substance use for young people in recovery (Anderson et al., 2007; Bryant et al., 2003; Hawkins, Catalano, & Miller, 1992; Resnick et al., 1997) while associated risk factors include a lack of academic success, availability of drugs, and interacting with substance-using individuals (Derzon, 2007; Finch & Wegman, 2012; Gonzales, Douglas, & Beattie, 2012; Svensson, 2000)—all of which commonly occur in or around the young person's school.

THE ROLE OF THE RECOVERY HIGH SCHOOL

The traditional high school environment creates two critical stressors that could initiate a relapse in the recovery process: academic stressors (that is, grades, discipline) and socialization stressors (that is, peer influences, social norms) (ARS, 2016; White & Finch, 2006). To minimize and control school-based stressors, recovery high schools were created with a dual mission to provide both quality education and recovery support to their students. Recovery high schools allow young people in recovery the opportunity for a high school environment surrounded by like-minded peers who share similar goals and experiences.

The first recovery high school was founded in Maryland in 1979 (Karakos, Finch, & Fisher, 2014), and like the recovery high schools of today, it operated like a traditional high school, where students return home at the end of the day. As of October 2022, the Association of Recovery Schools boasts nearly forty total schools, with seven of these schools having successfully received accreditation from the Association of Recovery Schools. Recovery high schools have a dual mission to provide both a high-quality education and recovery support services to young people in recovery from substance use disorders. These high schools provide a unique environment where young people can manage their substance use disorder recovery journey while maintaining academic progress, which evidence suggests may contribute to successful long-term sobriety (Gibson, 1997).

Hope Academy, a recovery high school located on the southside of Indianapolis, was founded in 2006. Hope offers students a "Core 40" Indiana High School diploma, as well as providing recovery supports to help them maintain their sobriety. Hope Academy is a small school: enrollment per year averages between thirty-five and forty-five students. The population of Hope Academy often skews toward the higher grades, with juniors and seniors often making up the majority of the student population. Special education students also make up a larger proportion of the student population when compared to statewide averages, with the current population of students with special needs at Hope Academy around 30 percent.

The Hope Academy Educational Model

Recovery high schools are tasked with providing students with recovery supports while also providing a rigorous high school education. The Hope Academy education model is based on ten principles by which the school develops community, provides recovery supports, and maintains the rigor of the educational content. While recovery high schools differ among themselves, many of the characteristics described here are common with other recovery high schools.

Principle I—*provide a recovery culture appropriate to high school–age students of diverse backgrounds.* The disease of chemical dependency does not discriminate. The demographics are clear; young people across diverse populations are affected by substance use disorders. Meeting the educational needs of these students demands that in every aspect of its operation, Hope Academy provides a safe, sober, and challenging high school experience, informed and driven by recovery values and processes that have been shown to motivate and support the sobriety and health of students, as well as to promote their educational success. To that end, Hope Academy provides staff with professional development in *cultural competency* and promotes an environment that respects students and their varied histories.

Principle II—*establish a school with recovery supports rather than a recovery center with educational supports.* Hope Academy places its primary focus on being a school while offering students support for their recovery from substance use. The primary responsibility of Hope Academy teachers is classroom instruction while staying informed and sensitive to individual student needs.

Principle III—*establish a code of conduct and discipline procedures based on restorative principles.* Because of the unique behavioral needs of many recovering students, behavior problems require attention through a responsive and restorative system, that is, a system that reinforces recovery values, enables the practice of recovery skills, develops a student's capacity to self-regulate, and helps the student engage self and others in civil and productive ways. To that end, Hope Academy has been implementing a school culture based on restorative practices for over ten years. The restorative practices being used at Hope Academy focus on building community, increasing self-awareness, and embracing the role that community plays in maintaining sobriety.

Principle IV—*provide students a state standards–based curriculum that balances critical content and relevant learning processes for the purpose of readying each student for post–high school life and further educational goals.* Hope Academy is in many ways a traditional high school—walk through the halls on a school day and the sounds of students changing classes, heading to lunch, or chatting with friends can be heard. Hope Academy also provides traditional guidance counseling for college and career and instruction focused on students gaining the skills needed to attain a level of success that will enable them to seek the form of post–high school education or a vocation that best fits their personal goals.

Principle V—*develop instructional delivery systems of various approaches to strategically promote active student engagement and diverse modes of learning.* An array of learning deficits has been associated with substance-impacted student status. Many students with substance use disorders show soft signs of varied cognitive impairments, insufficient for diagnosis but significant enough to challenge their school success. Hope Academy uses a variety of strategies and techniques to mitigate the effects of these impairments, for example, differentiated instruction, integrated thematic instruction, and hands-on learning. Proactive classroom management, interactive teaching, cooperative learning, and how to foster student social and emotional skill development are also the focus on professional development for the teaching staff to offset high-risk factors and increase academic achievement in populations prone to substance abuse.

Principle VI—*provide both external (standardized) and internal (nonstandardized) means to assess student achievement and to advance personalized learning.* As noted earlier, Hope Academy is a school that provides recovery supports, not a recovery center, with the goal of preparing students for college and career. To that end, staff and students at Hope Academy are held accountable in the same way that other high schools are held accountable. Hope implements an array of assessments to help teachers, students, and their families assess both academic progress and recovery success. The strategic and integrated use of external (standardized) assessments with internal (nonstandardized) assessments are used to gauge, from various perspectives, the academic, developmental, and recovery progress of each student. The school recognizes the necessity to use nonstandardized measures to maximize personalized learning, some of which may include projects, portfolios, résumés, presentations, etc. Students are given critical feedback and adjustment loops for guided growth in a context of personalized learning.

Principle VII—*provide students a variety of recovery supports and recovery requirements.* At Hope Academy recovery is part of the academic curriculum. Recovery coaches, school counselors, peer specialists, and the school nurse all work closely with the instructional staff to provide recovery support to students that focus on their ability to succeed in the classroom. As an example, Hope Academy provides a separate school environment for students who need additional education and recovery supports called STARR (Supportive, Therapeutic, Action-Focused Recovery Room). STARR is for new students who need time to acclimate to the unique structure and culture of Hope Academy and for current students who may need additional support in their recovery.

Principle VIII—*personalize each student's education by focusing on individual post–high school education and career plans.* Hope Academy provides students with guidance counseling in applying for college, exploring trade schools, enlisting in the military, and exploring other job areas.

Principle IX—*build an active professional development culture that demands constant professional reflection.* Hope Academy has built a professional development culture marked by collegiality, open faculty and staff exchange, information feedback systems, problem solving, and continuous professional education.

Principle X—*actively pursue alumni and adjunct community support to help the school fulfill its mission.* The recruitment and establishment of a wide range of community and individual collaborations supports student recovery, to broaden and enrich each student's academic experience, and to extend student service learning into the community.

APPLICATION OF THE HOPE ACADEMY TEN PRINCIPLES

Recovery support and recovery education is an important part of life at Hope Academy. Students participate in a schoolwide recovery circle twice a week, where students and staff share personal reflections on daily readings, goals, and accomplishments. Students also receive recovery education three days per week and have access to a recovery coach and peer specialists to discuss recovery plans and sobriety. Students who enter Hope Academy with little or no previous recovery education are placed in STARR (Supportive, Therapeutic, Action-Focused Recovery Room), a program that pulls students out of the regular community and gives them individualized academic time with each teacher, as well as a dedicated recovery education time with the recovery team. Hope Academy also provides students with the Serenity Room, where a student can recenter themselves in a calming environment.

Staff members at Hope Academy are trained in the area of adolescent substance use disorder, including brain function and trauma. Some of the strategies Hope Academy teachers use in teaching adolescents with substance use disorders include

- teaching lessons in small chunks,
- spiraling curriculum,
- applying learning to students' lives,
- assigning little to no homework,
- clearly posting the rules/expectations,
- creating horizontal lists instead of vertical lists, and
- providing students with a physical location where they can recenter themselves.

While it is the primary purpose of teachers to teach their classes, Hope Academy teachers are also trained in identifying issues and in funneling students to the appropriate supports. Hope Academy also employs a school nurse who performs drug screens, helps assess and meet student health needs, and addresses any other medical emergencies.

Hope Academy Discipline Plan

The most supportive learning environment for students in recovery from substance use disorders is one that is safe, is recovery focused, provides an environment where students *do not* encounter temptations by other students to use chemicals, and where students *do* receive support and encouragement from the education team and other students. Policies and procedures regarding behavior have been developed in a collaborative approach with the school staff. These policies are posted for all staff, students, and visitors to view as well as published and given to all students at the time of enrollment.

Because of the unique behavioral needs of many recovering students, student behavior problems are addressed through a responsive and restorative system (for example, a system that reinforces recovery values, enables the practice of recovery skills, develops student capacity to self-regulate, and helps the student engage self and others in civil and productive ways). This process, known as restorative justice, allows peer feedback on how the behavior is affecting the culture, focuses on repairing the harm that has been encountered, and then creates a plan to avoid the behavior in the future. This process brings the entire school together to confront the negative behavior and restore the recovery culture.

Hope Academy Curriculum

Hope Academy's curriculum is unique in that it is a combination of Core 40 classes based on both Indiana standards and recovery education. The Hope Academy philosophy is that it is first a school and second a recovery support system. The curriculum at Hope Academy embodies this philosophy through the implementation of a rigorous curriculum that includes recovery supports. Through the focus on seven main factors for success, Hope Academy provides students in recovery with both a rigorous education and a strong base for their recovery.

Factor I: Equivalent Validity with Continuous Progression. Substance abusing students have a history of being disconnected from their schools and suffering from a sense of alienation. The curricular experience presented to recovering students must help them replace their shame, doubt, and alienation by helping them successfully complete courses of recognizable similarity to those they experienced at their previous high schools, that is, a curriculum of equal rigor. This is why Hope Academy provides its students an Indiana Core 40–based curriculum in terms of identifiable core academic courses, general course content, standards, and accountability.

Factor II: Flexibility. Adolescents with substance abuse disorders share common issues around their addiction, but they are a diverse group with varied backgrounds, capacities, and aspirations. At Hope Academy, the curriculum is designed to acknowledge this fact. The Hope Academy curriculum provides students with (1) recovery courses that address universal recovery issues, (2) Core 40 academic courses that provide students with academic rigor, and (3) elective, flex, career-academic sequence, and service-learning courses that provide students with varied opportunities. The goal is to provide a curriculum with flexibility, so students can align their course of study to personal interests, background, capacities, and aspirations, whether those are college, career, or vocational.

Factor III: Meaning and Personal Relevance. To have a curriculum that truly engages recovering students, it must be viewed by students as relevant to their issues, interests, and life needs. Because Hope Academy is committed to a Core 40 basic curricular structure, its delivery requires unique and creative pedagogy that promotes student use of learning strategies to enhance their ability to construct knowledge in personally relevant ways. The curriculum at Hope Academy reflects the belief that a course's relevancy can be significantly increased through implementing an integrated thematic instruction design. This approach weaves relevant life situations, themes, and issues with the content and levels of mastery required by state standards.

For example, scholars have pointed out that alcohol and drug use is imbedded in the everyday fabric and historic flow of American life. Alcohol is a drug of everyday use; it occupies a special place in the social order that ties patterns of both use and abuse to regular life events—social intercourse, business exchange, courting, recreation, and leisure. In America, the ebb and flow of alcohol and drug abuse is dynamically interconnected with major events as well as with social, economic, moral, legal, and political issues of the day. Through thematic-integrated instruction, students see that their addiction problems are part of a line of ongoing American social and historic processes. They can then use this relevant template to organize and store in memory key historic events and processes.

Factor IV: Sufficient Integration and Scaffolding. Students recovering from chemical dependency will, in most cases, struggle with general dependency issues in other areas of their lives—school is usually one of those areas. Recovery high school educators are quick to point out that all too often recovering students are overwhelmed by feelings of helplessness and hopelessness when it comes to school. Years of negative interaction with teachers, behavior problems, low performance, and a nagging sense of failure haunt these youth. Hope Academy's curriculum is structured and integrated to build student competencies ("I can") and developmental assets ("I have") so that the recovering student's empty narcissism ("I haven't, but I'm still cool") and cooccurring helplessness and hopelessness ("I can't, and I never will") can be ameliorated. When a recovering student sees how academic course content can be used to enhance and support recovery and build personal capacities, his/her motivation and success in academic courses improves.

Factor V: Community Grounding. Addiction permeates and colors the whole life of a young person abusing substances. This fact tends to demarcate the difference between youth who *abuse* alcohol and other drugs and youth who are *addicted* to alcohol and other drugs. Central to addiction's "permeation" in a young person's life is the breaking of relationships—to self, loved ones, others, and, in general, to life. Repair of these breaks is essential for successful recovery. Helping adolescents with substance use disorders to recover requires much more than providing students a safe place away from peers who use and away from the temptation of substance supplies found in, around, and through school. A recovery school requires a sober community consciously pursuing the repair of relational breaks. The strong curriculum at Hope Academy ultimately facilitates learner engagement on numerous levels—self, others, and the environment. Thus, Hope Academy is committed to a school curriculum that promotes student interaction and community, a curriculum where students master academic requirements through strong bonds to individuals, school, and learning. For example, systems of instruction that emphasize isolated, individual learning, such as computerized learning, have a secondary or supportive role at Hope Academy. The central paradigm for instruction is human interaction.

Factor VI: Provision of Explicit and Implicit Recovery Management. Hope Academy integrates recovery management philosophy and core beliefs throughout its curriculum, as well as reflect this philosophy in the organizational design of the school and in the behavior and attitudes of faculty and staff. This is the *implicit* recovery management curriculum. To adequately support student recovery, though, a strong and continuous line of *explicit* recovery management courses must also be part of the curriculum. Consequently, integrated into the Hope Academy curriculum is a session at the beginning of the day to ensure students will start each day confronting the primary issue of their lives—their addiction—within the positive frame of recovery.

Factor VII: Data Driven Curriculum Evaluation and Adjustments. Hope Academy is committed to design and use continuous curriculum evaluations to inform pedagogy, and thereby provides students and families the tools for success in recovery and in attaining a high school diploma.

SPECIAL EDUCATION AT HOPE ACADEMY

The nature of the Hope Academy mission, and the special requirements of students in recovery from substance use disorders, places unique demands on the special education staff of the school. Specifically, students in recovery from substance use disorders are often diagnosed with both learning disabilities and mental health disorders that can impact their ability to succeed in high school. Their IEPs, mental health treatment plans, and recovery plans must align in order to provide the best possible educational outcomes for the student, requiring special education staff at Hope Academy to work at the intersection of special education, mental health, and addiction science.

CHARACTERISTICS OF HOPE ACADEMY STUDENTS WITH SPECIAL NEEDS

As noted previously, Hope Academy has a larger percentage of students with special needs than the state average. Many of the students arrive at Hope Academy with an IEP to ensure that they receive specialized instruction and related services. Their IEPs also require documentation of measurable growth and long-term goals and transition strategies. Fewer students arrive with a 504 plan to ensure that they receive effective accommodations to aid in their academic success and access to the learning environment but do not require specialized instruction. Students at Hope Academy may also have behavior intervention plans (BIPs), or a written improvement plan created based on the outcome of their functional behavior assessment. The behavior assessment identifies the cause of the challenging behavior, while the BIP specifies actions to be taken to replace or improve the behavior. All of these educational plans require yearly updates and are designed by a collaborative team of educators, parents, and mental health professionals.

Although they are a valuable tool in providing students with the supports they need to succeed, IEPs, 504s, and BIPs are not designed to specifically address the issues of adolescents with substance use disorders. In fact, the IEPs provided to Hope Academy when a student enrolls do not include an acknowledgment of a substance use disorder, and only a subset of them include a mental health diagnosis. Because all Hope Academy students are struggling with a substance use disorder, even those students whose constellation of symptoms do not reach the level of a mental health diagnosis require mental health supports.

To ensure that students with special needs receive the appropriate mental health supports, the special education staff, teaching staff, and recovery staff work together to use the supports available to all Hope Academy students as part of the special education process. To do this they explicitly incorporate aspects of the Hope Academy model already in place (for example, the STARR Room and the Serenity Room) into the goals of the student's learning plan. Thus, Hope Academy students with special needs can have visits to the Serenity Room written into their IEP, 504, or behavior plan. Use of the Serenity Room, and the recentering activities that occur there, can also be included in the goals of a student's IEP. The use of specific goals to address the mental health of students with special needs allows the Hope Academy staff to use the structure of the IEP to make the mental health accommodations concrete and operationalized.

An additional use of the IEP is to address the impact of the substance use disorder itself as well as the medications used to treat the disorder. The impact of long-term substance use on the adolescent brain can manifest itself both socially and cognitively. Further, the medications prescribed to help a student maintain their sobriety can also lead to changes in their cognitive abilities, often temporarily impacting their cognitive abilities. The learning plans of Hope Academy students with special needs can reflect the needed academic and mental health scaffolds and supports to ensure that their learning continues. Because the effects of the medications may be temporary, either because the student is acclimating to the drugs or because they were prescribed for a short period of time, the regular updates required of a learning plan such as an IEP ensures that the student's needs are being met in the near term but allows for modifications over the long term.

The links between mental health, maintaining recovery, and academic success are explicitly acknowledged at Hope Academy. The complexity of these interactions is why the special education staff rely on quality student information to help Hope Academy students with special needs succeed. To ensure that students are seen in all the different contexts that make up the day of a Hope Academy student—academic, social, and recovery—all the professionals who impact students are asked to share their view of the student. All of these efforts come together during the learning plan case conference meetings. At Hope Academy the recovery coach and, if possible, any additional therapists treating the student will attend. For those students with a mental health diagnosis, Hope Academy encourages their treatment providers to attend and share their knowledge of the student during these meetings. Mental health professionals are given time during the IEP or BIP meeting to share their knowledge of the student and are given the opportunity to provide input into the academic and behavioral interventions and supports that the student will receive and the learning and behavioral goals set. Mental health and recovery staff also provide mental health supports during this meeting, acting as a trusted person who has a therapeutic, rather than an academic, relationship with the student in what may be perceived by the student as a stressful situation. The ultimate goal of the meeting is to have the entire group of educational and mental health professionals working with the student, their family, and each other to ensure that all parties are moving together to improve the educational and recovery outcomes of the student.

The inclusive nature of these meetings also applies to the recovery success of the student. Special educators attend meetings held to tailor the recovery supports provided by Hope Academy to each students' needs. This collaborative process is evident in the meetings that occur after a student has a return to use episode. At Hope Academy, when a student has an episode of returning to substance use, the student is required to self-report the episode and then work with the Hope Academy leadership, teaching, and recovery staff to determine what led to the return to use, the cognitive and emotional reasons for the return to use, and then work to determine how the student will make amends to the Hope Academy community (as required by the restorative practices used to support the school culture). As part of the team of professionals working toward student success, the special educators are part of these meetings. The underlying reason for the inclusion of special education in these meetings is simple: when the student, family, and Hope Academy staff design a plan to help the student through their return to use, everyone who is supporting the student in their recovery needs to be part of the plan.

The mission of Hope Academy is to provide a safe, sober, restorative, and challenging school experience for high school students recovering from alcoholism and/or drug addiction who have made a commitment to personal recovery, have a desire to learn, want to attain a high school diploma, and are willing to be an active part of a school community of like-minded students and faculty. The nature of the Hope Academy mission, and of the student body, places unique demands on the special education staff of the school. Specifically, students in recovery from substance use disorders are often struggling with both learning disabilities and mental health disorders that can impact their ability to succeed in high school. Their learning plans, mental health treatment, and recovery plans must align in order to provide the best possible educational outcomes for the student, requiring special education staff at Hope Academy to work at the intersection of special education, mental health, and addiction science.

REFERENCES

Anderson, K. G., Ramo, D. E., Schulte, M. T., Cummins, K., & Brown, S. A. (2007). Substance use treatment outcomes for youth: Integrating personal and environmental predictors. *Drug and Alcohol Dependence, 88*(1): 42–48. https://doi.org/10.1016/j.drugalcdep.2006.09.014.

ARS (2016). *The State of Recovery High Schools, 2016 Biennial Report.* Decton, TX: Association of Recovery Schools.

Botzet, A. M., McIlvaine, P. W., Winters, K. C., Fanhorst, T., & Dittel, C. (2014). Data collection strategies and measurement tools for assessing academic and therapeutic outcomes in recovery schools. *Peabody Journal of Education, 89*(2): 197–213. https://doi.org/10.1080/0161956X.2014.895648.

Breda, C., & Heflinger, C. A. (2004). Predicting incentives to change among adolescents with substance abuse disorder. *The American Journal of Drug and Alcohol Abuse, 30*(2): 251–67. https://doi.org/10.1081/ADA-120037377.

Brown, S. A., & Tapert, S. F. (2004). Adolescence and the trajectory of alcohol use: Basic to clinical studies. *Annals of the New York Academy of Sciences, 1021*(1): 234–44. https://doi.org/10.1196/annals.1308.028.

Bryant, A. L., Schulenberg, J. E., O'Malley, P. M., Bachman, J. G., & Johnston, L. D. (2003). How academic achievement, attitudes, and behaviors relate to the course of substance use during adolescence: A 6-year, multiwave national longitudinal study. *Journal of Research on Adolescence, 13*(3): 361–97. https://doi.org/10.1111/1532-7795.1303005.

Chambers, R. A., Taylor, J. R., & Potenza, M. N. (2003). Developmental neurocircuitry of motivation in adolescence: a critical period of addiction vulnerability. *American Journal of Psychiatry.* https://doi.org/10.1176/appi.ajp.160.6.1041.

Cobb, S. (1976). Social support as a moderator of life stress. *Psychosomatic Medicine, 38*(5), 300–314. https://doi.org/10.1097/00006842-197609000-00003.

Cohen, P., Chen, H., Crawford, T. N., Brook, J. S., & Gordon, K. (2007). Personality disorders in early adolescence and the development of later substance use disorders in the general population. *Drug and Alcohol Dependence, 88*: S71–S84. https://doi.org/10.1016/j.drugalcdep.2006.12.012.

Dennis, M., Babor, T. F., Roebuck, M. C., & Donaldson, J. (2002). Changing the focus: The case for recognizing and treating cannabis use disorders. *Addiction, 97*(s1): 4–15. https://doi.org/10.1046/j.1360-0443.97.s01.10.x.

Derzon, J. H. (2007). Using correlational evidence to select youth for prevention programming. *The Journal of Primary Prevention, 28*(5): 421–47. DOI: 10.1007/s10935-007-0107-7.

Fairbanks (2016). Recovery high school. www.fairbankscd.org/program/recovery-high-school/.

Finch, A., & Wegman, H. (2012). Recovery high schools: Opportunities for support and personal growth for students in recovery. *The Prevention Researcher, 19*(5): 12–17.

French, M. T., Popovici, I., & Tapsell, L. (2008). The economic costs of substance abuse treatment: Updated estimates and cost bands for program assessment and reimbursement. *Journal of Substance Abuse Treatment, 35*(4): 462–69. https://doi.org/10.1016/j.jsat.2007.12.008.

Gibson, B. (1997). An introduction to the controversy over tobacco. *Journal of Social Issues, 53*(1), 3–11. https://doi.org/10.1111/0022-4537.219972.

Gonzales, R., Douglas, A. M., & Beattie, R. (2012). Understanding recovery barriers: Youth perceptions about substance use relapse. *American Journal of Health Behavior, 36*(5): 602–14. https://doi.org/10.5993/AJHB.36.5.3.

Hawkins, J. D., Catalano, R. F., & Miller, J. Y. (1992). Risk and protective factors for alcohol and other drug problems in adolescence and early adulthood: Implications for substance abuse prevention. *Psychological Bulletin, 112*(1): 64–105.

Homel, J., Thompson, K., and Leadbeater, B. (2014). Trajectories of marijuana use in youth ages 15–25: Implications for postsecondary education experiences. *Journal of Studies on Alcohol and Drugs, 75*(4): 674–83. https://doi.org/10.15288/jsad.2014.75.674.

Jainchill, N. (2012). *Understanding and treating adolescent substance use disorders.* Civic Research Institute.

Johnston, L. D., O'Malley, P. M., & Bachman, J. G. (2010). Monitoring the future: National results on adolescent drug use. Overview of key findings, 2009. *NIH Publication No. 10-7583*. National Institutes of Health.

Kann, L., Kinchen, S. A., Williams, B. I., Ross, J. G., Lowry, R., Grunbaum, J. A., & Kolbe, L. J. (2000). Center for Disease Control and Prevention. Youth risk behavioral surveillance–United States. *CDC Surveillance Summaries, 49*: 22–25.

Karakos, H., Finch, A., & Fisher, E. (2014). Accessing recovery: An ecological analysis of barriers and opportunities for adolescents through recovery high schools, in Biennial Meeting of the Society for Research on Adolescence. Austin, TX.

Larm, P., Hodgins, S., Larsson, A., Samuelson, Y. M., & Tengstrom, A. (2008). Long-term outcomes of adolescents treated for substance misuse. *Drug and Alcohol Dependence, 96*(1): 79–89. https://doi.org/10.1016/j.drugalcdep.2008.01.026.

Lisdahl, K. M., Wright, N. E., Medina-Kirchner, C., Maple, K. E., & Shollenbarger, S. (2014). Considering cannabis: The effects of regular cannabis use on neurocognition in adolescents and young adults. *Current Addiction Reports, 1*(2): 144–56. DOI: 10.1007/s40429-014-0019-6.

McLellan, A. T., Lewis, D. C., O'Brien, C. P., & Kleber, H. D. (2000). Drug dependence, a chronic medical illness: Implications for treatment, insurance, and outcomes evaluation. *Journal of the American Medical Association, 284*(13): 1689–95. DOI:10.1001/jama.284.13.1689.

Menasco, M. A., & Blair, S. L. (2014). Adolescent substance use and marital status in adulthood. *Journal of Divorce & Remarriage, 55*(3): 216–38. https://doi.org/10.1080/10502556.2014.887382.

Nash, A., & Collier, C. (2016). The alternative peer group: A developmentally appropriate recovery support model for adolescents. *Journal of Addictions Nursing, 27*(2): 109–19. DOI: 10.1097/JAN.0000000000000122.

Newcomb, M. D., & Bentler, P. M. (1988). Impact of adolescent drug use and social support on problems of young adults: A longitudinal study. *Journal of Abnormal Psychology, 97*(1): 64–75. https://doi.org/10.1037/0021-843X.97.1.64.

NIDA (2014). *Principles of adolescent substance use disorder treatment: A research-based guide.* https://nida.nih.gov/publications/principles-adolescent-substance-use-disorder-treatment-research-based-guide/director.

Patrick, M. E., Schulenberg, J. E., & O'Malley, P. M. (2013). High school substance use as a predictor of college attendance, completion, and dropout: A national multicohort longitudinal study. *Youth & Society, 48*(3). https://doi.org/10.1177/0044118X13508961.

Resnick, M. D., Bearman, P. S., Blum, R. W., Bauman, K. E., Harris, K. M., Jones, J., Tabor, J., Beuhring, T., Sieving, R. E., Shrew, M., Ireland, M., Bearinger, L. H., & Udry, J. R. (1997). Protecting adolescents from harm: Findings from the National Longitudinal Study on Adolescent Health. *Jama, 278*(10): 823–32. doi:10.1001/jama.1997.03550100049038.

Sacks, J. J., Gonzales, K. R., Bouchery, E. E., Tomedi, L. E., & Brewer, R. D. (2015). 2010 national and state costs of excessive alcohol consumption. *American Journal of Preventive Medicine, 49*(5): e73–e79. https://doi.org/10.1016/j.amepre.2015.05.031.

Salzer, M. S. (2002). Consumer-delivered services as a best practice in mental health care delivery and the development of practice guidelines. *Mental Health Association of Southeastern Pennsylvania Best Practices Team Philadelphia*, 355–82. DOI: 10.1080/10973430208408443.

Squeglia, L. M., Jacobus, J., & Tapert, S. F. (2009).The influence of substance use on adolescent brain development. *Clinical EEG and Neuroscience, 40*(1): 31–38. https://doi.org/10.1177/155005940904000110.

Substance Abuse and Mental Health Services Administration (2021). *Key substance use and mental health indicators in the United States: Results from the 2020 National Survey on Drug Use and Health (HHS Publication No. PEP21-07-01-003, NSDUH Series H-56)*. Rockville, MD: Center for Behavioral Health Statistics and Quality, Substance Abuse and Mental Health Services Administration. https://www.samhsa.gov/data/.

Substance Abuse and Mental Health Services Administration, Center for Behavioral Health Statistics and Quality (2013). *The CBHSQ report: A day in the life of American adolescents: Substance use facts update.* Rockville, MD. https://www.samhsa.gov/data/.

Svensson, R. (2000). Risk factors for different dimensions of adolescent drug use. *Journal of Child & Adolescent Substance Abuse, 9*(3): 67–90. https://doi.org/10.1300/J029v09n03_05.

Thoma, R. J., Monnig, M. A., Lysne, P. A., Ruhl, D. A., Pommy, J. A., Bogenschutz, M., Tonigan, J. S., & Yeo, R. A. (2011). Adolescent substance abuse: The effects of alcohol and marijuana on neuropsychological performance. *Alcoholism: Clinical and Experimental Research, 35*(1): 39–46. https://doi.org/10.1111/j.1530-0277.2010.01320.x.

Vaillant, G. E. (1988). What can long-term follow-up teach us about relapse and prevention of relapse in addiction? *British Journal of Addiction, 83*(10): 1147–57. https://doi.org/10.1111/j.1360-0443.1988.tb03021.x.

White, W., & Finch, A. (2006). The recovery school movement: Its history and future. *Counselor, 7*(2): 54–57.

Whiteford, H. A., Degenhardt, L., Rehm, J., Baxter, A. J., Ferrari, A. J., Erskine, H. E., Charlson, F. J., Norman, R. E., Flazman, A. D., Johns, N., Murray, C. J., & Vos, T. (2013). Global burden of disease attributable to mental and substance use disorders: Findings from the Global Burden of Disease Study 2010. *The Lancet, 382*(9904): 1575–86. https://doi.org/10.1016/S0140-6736(13)61611-6.

Winters, K. C., Stinchfield, R. D., Opland, E., Weller, C., & Latimer, W. W. (2000). The effectiveness of the Minnesota Model approach in the treatment of adolescent drug abusers. *Addiction, 95*(4): 601–612. https://doi.org/10.1046/j.1360-0443.2000.95460111.x.

Young, S., Corley, R. P., Stallings, M. C., Rhee, S. H., Crowley, T. J., & Hewitt, J. K. (2002). Substance use, abuse and dependence in adolescence: prevalence, symptom profiles and correlates. *Drug and Alcohol Dependence, 68*(3): 309–22. https://doi.org/10.1016/S0376-8716(02)00225-9.

Index

Page numbers in *italics* refer to figures and textboxes.

absenteeism, 53, 110, 116; chronic absenteeism, 98, 99, 119; chronic illness and, 88, 89, 100, 101, 103, 105; prolonged absences, expecting and planning for, 10; risks of being absent, 52, 87; socialization challenges due to, 90, 92, 100
Academic Health Cliff, 15, 22–23, 24, 25
accommodations and modifications, 1, 8, 14, 67; 504 plans providing, 2, 3, 117, 139, 140; IEP sections on, 4, 5–6, 7; for students with chronic illness, 90, 92, 96–97, 100
addiction, 137, 138, 139, 141, 142
ADHD/ADD, 2, 32, *121*
adolescence, 87; common illnesses in, 88–92; substance abuse during, 130–31, 135, 137, 138, 140
African American students, 18, 20, 28, *49*; medication dosage visits to school nurses, 34, *35,* 37; risk factors for, *50–51,* 52; in special education classes, 16–17
alcohol, 41, 130, 137, 138, 141
allergies and allergens, 2, 88, 119–20
American Public Health Association, 19

Americans with Disabilities Act Amendments Act (2008), 117
anaphylaxis, treating, 120
anger management, 41
anxiety, 8, 21, 44, 70–71, *93,* 120, 123
asthma, 2, 40, 45, 88, *93,* 102, 103–4, 120–21
attendance, 40, 45, 53, 74, *81,* 98; chronic illness, impact on, 88, 102, 104; education funds as tied to, 99; IEP students and inconsistent attendance, 72–73; pandemic, attendance-taking challenges during, 76, 82, 83–84; school nurse presence and improved attendance, 109, 119
Autism Spectrum Disorder (ASD), 41, 94, 121

basic skills development (BSD) model, 77, *81*
behavioral needs, 6, 17, 36, 42, 44, 99, 133; BIPS, needs addressed in, 139–41; Hope Academy, taking needs into account, 136, 141; school-based health centers, aid from, 40, 41
the brain, 94, 130, 135, 140

147

Budde, Ray, 15–16
Building Dreams Platform, 47, 53
bullying, 42, 43, 126

Cambrian Clearsight, 20–22, *23*, 24
cancer, 18, 88, 91–92, *93*
Canvas (virtual learning platform), 83–84
cardiac conditions, *93*
CARES Act, 63
Certified Pediatric Nurses (CPNs), 116
charter schools, 15–16, 18–19, 20, 25
chronic illnesses, 40; common types of, 88–92, *93*; educational situations for students with, 94–99; educators, implications for, 102–4; pediatric chronic illness, defining, 87–88; school reentry for students with, 99–102, 105
clustering, 47, *48*
cognitive behavioral therapy, 36, 44
college, 116, 133, 134, 135, 137
confidentiality, 10, *113,* 118
Consortium for Health Education, Economic Empowerment, and Research (CHEER), 19–20
COVID-19, 27, 29, 63, 72, 80, 86; design thinking and, 61, 62; high school perspective, 73–78; recovery efforts, education community as supporting, 15, 25; teachers' perspectives on, 66–68, 82; virtual learning during pandemic, 69–73
curriculum, 5, 39, 43, 67, 135; accommodations to the academic curriculum, 96, *97*; COVID-19 pandemic as affecting, 68; Hope Academy curriculum, 136–39; recovery as part of, 134; TSS, holistic curriculum of, 27, 28
cystic fibrosis (CF), 89–90, *93,* 94, 101

diabetes, 2, 88, 90–91, *93,* 110, 111, *112,* 122
disabilities, 3, *12,* 25, 41, 46, 63, 88; IEPs as accommodating, 4, 5–6, 10, 63, 94; Individuals with Disabilities Education Act, 17, 87, 94–95, 117; learning disabilities and substance abuse, 130, 139, 142; least restrictive environments and, 7–8; legal determination of child disability, 1–2; NSE, students with disabilities at, 18–19, 20; Section 504 as protecting students with, 2, 95, 117
disorders, 32, 121; blood disorders, 88, *93*; epilepsy as a seizure disorder, 122–23; psychiatric disorders, 41, 92; substance use disorders, 129, 132, 133, 136, 139, 141–42; US, prevalence of disorders in, 130–31
drug screenings, 136

"Education by Charter" (Budde), 15–16
Elementary and Secondary Education Act (ESEA), 17
elementary school (K–5/K–6), 20, 27, 47, 52
Endrew F. v. Douglas County School District, 95
English as a new language (ENL), 28, 35
English language arts (ELA), 21–23, 24, *74,* 83
English language learners (ELs/ELLs), 64, 67–68, 74, 76–77, 84
epilepsy, *121,* 122–23
EPPSP Blueprint 2020 (Lecklider), 61, 62, 69
Every Student Succeeds Act (ESSA), 17–18, 67
Experiential Program for Preparing School Principals (EPPSP), 61, 62–64

Family Educational Rights and Privacy Act (FERPA), 103, 117, 118
fidgets, access to, 97
Flipgrid, 68
follow up, 40, *115*
free appropriate public education (FAPE), 6, 95

General Education Intervention (GEI), 17
Google Classroom, 68, 70
grades and academic standards, 9, 82, 87, 98, 131, 132
grammar school (K–8), 18, 20
G-tubes, 124

health care visits (HCVs): special education and, 32–36, 37–38; TSS dataset on, 28–32. *See also* school nurses
Health Insurance Portability and Accountability Act (HIPAA), 72, 103, 118
Health Level of Supports sample, *12–13*
Henry Street Settlement, 109–10, 114
high school: absenteeism during, 98, 99; charter high schools, 19, 20; COVID-19, high school perspective on, 73–78; Hope Academy, ten principles applied at, 135–39; recovery high schools, 129, 132–35, 141–42; substance use disorders, role of high school in, 131
Hispanic students, 18, 20, 28, *35*, 77; in Indiana schools, 73–74; risk factors for, *49–51*
Hope Academy, 129; educational model, 132–35; special needs students at, 139–42; ten principles of, 135–39
Hospital Educator and Academic Liaison (HEAL) Association, 100
hybrid instruction, 67–68, 75–78, 80–85
hypoglycemia, managing, 91, *113*

Ignite Achievement Academy, 28, 30
individualized education programs (IEPS), 19, 25, 32, 63, 95, 117, 125; accommodations and modifications for, 96; attendance concerns for students with, 72–73; eligibility determinants, 1–2, 4–6, 94; health data leveraged on behalf of students with, 15, 16; at Hope Academy, 139–42; Latin American students with, 74; medical needs, IEP points for students with, 9–10; purpose of the IEP, 3–4; reevaluation process, 8–9; school nurses, including in IEP meetings, 116, 118, 126; students with chronic illness and, 87, 97, 104; support for general education teachers in, 6–7; targeted goals, developing, 110–11
individualized health care plan (IHP), *112*, 124
Individuals with Disabilities Education Act (IDEA), 17, 63, 87, 94–95, 96, 117
intermittent hypoxia, 89
intervention, 16, 21, 24, 42, 78, *79*, 126; behavior intervention plans, 139–41; behavior interventions, 17, 139, 141; CHEER platform, guide intervention data tracked in, 20; early intervention, 17, 39, 117; in hybrid learning situations, 84–85; IHPs, sample interventions for, *112–13*; in machine learning model, 52–53; mental health interventions, 43–44; school nurse interventions, 110–11
ISTEP test, 19, *73–74*

Jamboard, 68
juvenile idiopathic arthritis (JIA), *93*

K–12 schools, 20, 61
Kahoot, 68

Lake, Robin, 16
Latino students. *See* Hispanic students
least restrictive environment, 7–8
Lecklider, Debra, 61
leukemia, 91–92, *93*, 94, 104
lice, 21, 40
lockdowns, 42, 91

machine learning case study, 40, 46–52, 55
medical device and procedure needs, 123–24

mental health, 39, 111, 123, 129; Hope Academy, mental health at, 139–42; school-based mental health centers, 40–41; Tier 2 strategies for, 43–44; Tier 3 services for, 45–46
mentoring, 42, 44–45
middle school, 20, 76, 98, 110
mobility devices, 124
Moodle, 68
multiracial students, 18, 20, 28, *35, 49–51*
multitiered systemic system of support (MTSS), 25, 66; as an evolving approach, 16–18; PHDP example, 20, 23–24; Tier 1 strategies, 39, 40–43, 52; Tier 2 strategies, 39–40, 42, 43–45, 52–53, 55; Tier 3 strategies, 39–40, 42, 45–46, 53
Murphy, Hardy, 16

National Association of School Nurses (NASN), 114, *115*
National Center on Special Education in Charter Schools, 19
national licensure exam (NCLEX), 116, 118
Nationally Certified School Nurses (NCSNs), 116
No Child Left Behind Act (NCLB), 17–18, 67
Northwest Evaluation Association Measures of Academic Progress (NWEA MAP), 28, 29, 30, 35–36
Nowland Schools of Excellence (NSE), 18–19, 20, 22–25
nurses. *See* school nurses

Office for Civil Rights (OCR), 95–96, 98
Office of Special Education and Rehabilitative Services, 96
ostomy, 124
other health impairments (OHI), 94

Paramount Health Data Project (PHDP), 20–24

peer relations, 7, 44, 53, 86, 95, 102, 131, 136, 138; chronic absences, effect upon, 52, 87, 98; medical conditions as affecting, 90, 103, 104, 111; peer mediation, 41, 42; peer specialists, recovery support from, 134, 135; peer support reentry programs, 100, 101; in recovery high schools, 132; in School Day Needs Assessment chart, *14*
predictors, 98, 101
pregnant youth, 40
prevention, 41, 44, *115*

recovery: Hope Academy, services for, 135–39, 140–42; recovery high schools, 129, 132–35; students in recovery, 130–31
registered nurses (RNs), 116. *See also* school nurses
Rehabilitation Act of 1973, 2, 95, 117
relapse, 132
Response to Intervention (RTI), 17, 66
risk, 22, 27, 41, *54,* 98, *115,* 131, 134; chronic illness, risks for students with, 87, 89, 91, 92, *93,* 95, 100, 101; high-risk students, 47, 53, 55; machine learning case study on, 40, *50–52*; PHDP, at-risk students in, 20, 21, 23
Rogers, Lina, 110, 118

safety-oriented strategies, 42
school-based health centers, 39, 40–41, 45
School Day Needs Assessment sample, *14*
school nurses, 27, 66, 104, 117, 134, 136; academics, impact of nurse visits on, 65, 118–19; Cambium Clearsight on visits to, 20–22; educators, implications of nursing process for, 110–111; Framework for 21st Century School Nursing Practice, 114–16, *115*; history of school nursing, 109–10; in MTSS process, 15, 16, 24; partnerships

with, 102–3, 125–26; role in educating students with health concerns, 119–25; in school-based health centers, 40, 45; special education students and, 32–37; TSS data on school nurse visits, 28–32

school reentry process, 87, 99, 100, 101–2, 105

Section 504 plans, 10, 25, 117, 139; describing and defining, 2, 3; health data leveraged on behalf of students with, 15, 16; at Hope Academy, 139, 140; Office for Civil Rights as regulating, 95–96; school nurses, including in 504 meetings, 116, 118, 126; students with chronic illness and, 87, 91, 92, 97, 104

seizures, 91, *93,* 122–23, 126

sickle cell anemia (SCA), 88, *93,* 94

sleep, 21, 40, 89, *121,* 122

social and emotional learning (SEL) programs, 41

special education, 19, 62, 96, 129; African American students in, 16–17; at charter schools, 15–16; chronic illness, for students with, 91, 92, 94, 102, 104; COVID-19 effect on, 25, 63–64, 67–74, 77–78; HCVs and, 29, 30–38; at Hope Academy, 132, 139–42; hybrid schedules for, 77, 84; IEP qualifications and, 1–2, 3, 4; least restrictive environment as a main tenet of, 7–8; PHDP data regarding, 20, 24; Section 504 and, 2, 10, 95, 117

special needs, 16, 36, 117; Hope Academy, students with special needs at, 132, 139–42; pandemic challenges, 67–68; school nurse visits of children with special needs, 32, 33

substance abuse, 17, 41, 134; in adolescence, 130–31, 135, 137, 138, 140; substance use disorders, 129, 132, 133, 136, 139, 141–42; truancy as linked with, 99

support, 17, 43, 52, 65, 72, 78, 86, 99, 101, *121;* academic support, 18, 19, 24, 44; chronic illnesses, supporting students with, 87, *93, 102;* ELL students, providing support to, 67–68, 77; face-to-face support, 76; health level of supports, *12;* in hybrid environments, 80, 81, 84–85; IEPs providing, 1, 6–7, 10, 140–41; in MTSS process, 15, 24, 39; in Paramount Health Data Project, 20, 21; in recovery high schools, 129, 132–35, 136, 138, 141; safety-oriented strategies for, 42; school nurses, support from, 111, *113,* 125; special education support, 16, 63, 67, 71

Supportive, Therapeutic, Action-Focused Recovery Room (STARR), 134, 135, 140

The Scholar School (TSS), 27–32

tracheotomy tube, 124

transition readiness, 125

trauma, 61, 62, 69, 123, 135; of financially marginalized students, 65; Tier 3 services and, 45; trauma-informed practices, 42–43, 44

truancy. *See* absenteeism

urinary catheters, 124

US Department of Education (USDOE), 19, 98

violence, 39, 42, 43, 53

Westfield High School, 77

wheelchairs, 124

white students, 18, 20, 28, *35, 49–51,* 53, 74

Zoom classes, 68, 70, 82, 83–84

About the Editors

Azure D. S. Angelov earned a PhD in special education and multicultural education from Indiana University, Bloomington. Additionally, Dr. Angelov completed the High Potential Leaders Executive Education Program at the Harvard Business School. Dr. Angelov served as associate professor of special education at the University of Indianapolis and has earned numerous professional awards. She serves as CEO for the Paramount Health Data Project.

Mary Jo Rattermann received her PhD in cognitive development from the University of Illinois at Urbana–Champaign. She has expertise in experimental methodologies, advanced statistics, and evaluative procedures. Dr. Rattermann was a research associate at the Center of Excellence in Leadership of Learning (CELL) at the University of Indianapolis, where she was also adjunct faculty in the School of Education. Dr. Rattermann currently serves as an evaluator and director of research for the Paramount Health Data Project.

www.ingramcontent.com/pod-product-compliance
Lightning Source LLC
Chambersburg PA
CBHW070359240426
43671CB00013BA/2566